The Biggest Wars in History

CRAFTED BY SKRIUWER

Copyright © 2024 by Skriuwer.

All rights reserved. No part of this book may be used or reproduced in any form whatsoever without written permission except in the case of brief quotations in critical articles or reviews.

At **Skriuwer**, we're more than just a team—we're a global community of people who love books. In Frisian, "Skriuwer" means "writer," and that's at the heart of what we do: creating and sharing books with readers worldwide. Wherever you are in the world, **Skriuwer** is here to inspire learning.

Frisian is one of the oldest languages in Europe, closely related to English and Dutch, and is spoken by about **500,000 people** in the province of **Friesland** (Fryslân), located in the northern Netherlands. It's the second official language of the Netherlands, but like many minority languages, Frisian faces the challenge of survival in a modern, globalized world.

We're using the money we earn to promote the Frisian language.

For more information, contact : **kontakt@skriuwer.com** (www.skriuwer.com)

Disclaimer:
The images in this book are creative reinterpretations of historical scenes. While every effort was made to accurately capture the essence of the periods depicted, some illustrations may include artistic embellishments or approximations. They are intended to evoke the atmosphere and spirit of the times rather than serve as precise historical records.

TABLE OF CONTENTS

CHAPTER 1: EARLY WARFARE AND THE DAWN OF ORGANIZED ARMIES

- Emergence of small-scale clan conflicts and the roots of organized violence
- Transition from nomadic groups to settled societies and the need for defense
- First recorded wars in Mesopotamia and the development of bronze weapons
- Rise of standing armies, mercenaries, and religious justification for warfare

CHAPTER 2: THE RISE AND FALL OF MESOPOTAMIAN AND EGYPTIAN POWERS

- Akkadian Empire under Sargon and early imperial models
- Third Dynasty of Ur, Babylon under Hammurabi, and the spread of law codes
- Unification of Egypt, Old and Middle Kingdom militaries, and the creation of fortifications
- New Kingdom expansion, the role of chariots, and growing rivalries with neighboring powers

CHAPTER 3: THE GRECO-PERSIAN STRUGGLES

- Persian Empire's vast expansion and Greek city-states' independent spirit
- Ionian Revolt and its impact on Athens and Eretria
- Key battles: Marathon, Thermopylae, Salamis, and Plataea
- Consequences for Greek unity, cultural identity, and later power shifts in the Aegean

CHAPTER 4: THE WARS OF ALEXANDER THE GREAT AND THE HELLENISTIC WORLD

- Macedonia's rise under Philip II and Alexander's inheritance
- Conquest of the Persian Empire: major battles (Granicus, Issus, Gaugamela)
- Alexander's campaigns in Egypt, Mesopotamia, and beyond
- Fragmentation of the empire after Alexander's death and the formation of Hellenistic states

CHAPTER 5: THE PUNIC WARS

- Rome and Carthage's competition for dominance in the western Mediterranean
- First Punic War: naval innovations and Rome's eventual victory
- Hannibal's campaigns in the Second Punic War, including the Alps crossing
- Rome's ultimate triumph in the Third Punic War and the destruction of Carthage

---

CHAPTER 6: THE ROMAN CIVIL WARS AND IMPERIAL EXPANSION

- Growing tensions in the late Roman Republic: the Gracchi, Marius, and Sulla
- Julius Caesar's rise, the First Triumvirate, and the Gallic Wars
- Caesar's dictatorship, assassination, and the resultant power struggles
- Octavian (Augustus), the end of the Republic, and the birth of the Roman Empire

---

CHAPTER 7: THE WARS OF THE MIDDLE AGES (PART 1) — BYZANTIUM, THE RISE OF ISLAM, AND THE EARLY CRUSADES

- Continuation of the Eastern Roman (Byzantine) Empire after the West's fall
- Rapid expansion of Islamic caliphates and ensuing Byzantine-Islamic clashes
- Rise of Charlemagne's Frankish realm and the fragmentation following his death
- Call for the First Crusade: motivations, People's Crusade, and the capture of Jerusalem

---

CHAPTER 8: THE WARS OF THE MIDDLE AGES (PART 2) — LATE CRUSADES, MONGOL INVASIONS, AND EUROPEAN FEUDAL CONFLICTS

- Later Crusades in the Levant and the diversion of the Fourth Crusade to Constantinople
- Mongol conquests under Genghis Khan
- Feudal warfare in Europe, the evolution of knights, and the role of castles
- Changing power structures and the eventual decline of the crusading movement

CHAPTER 9: THE HUNDRED YEARS' WAR

- Dynastic disputes over the French crown between England and France
- Early English successes with the longbow (Crécy, Poitiers)
- Joan of Arc's leadership and the eventual French resurgence
- Effects on English and French national identities and the rise of professional armies

---

CHAPTER 10: THE WARS OF THE ROSES

- Internal conflict in England between the houses of Lancaster and York
- Key battles: St Albans, Wakefield, Towton, and Tewkesbury
- Edward IV's rise, Richard III's controversial reign, and the final victory of Henry Tudor
- Creation of the Tudor dynasty and the end of Plantagenet rule

---

CHAPTER 11: THE OTTOMAN EXPANSION AND CONFLICTS IN EASTERN EUROPE

- Rise of the Ottoman Empire from a small beylic to a major power
- Conquests in the Balkans, the fall of Constantinople (1453), and subsequent wars
- Struggles against Hungary, Venice, and the Habsburgs; siege warfare like Vienna (1529, 1683)
- Systems of governance (millets, devshirme) and the empire's multi-ethnic nature

---

CHAPTER 12: THE THIRTY YEARS' WAR

- Religious and dynastic tensions in the Holy Roman Empire after the Reformation
- Bohemian revolt, Danish and Swedish interventions, and France's entrance against the Habsburgs
- Devastation of German lands, mass population losses, and eventual Peace of Westphalia (1648)
- Emergence of the balance-of-power concept and the modern state system

CHAPTER 13: THE WARS OF LOUIS XIV AND SHIFTING EUROPEAN ALLIANCES

- French ambition under the Sun King, standing armies, and mercantilist policies
- War of Devolution, Dutch War, Nine Years' War, and War of the Spanish Succession
- Key battles (Blenheim, Ramillies, Malplaquet) and central figures (Marlborough)
- Rise of Britain as a maritime power, the consolidation of Bourbon power in Spain, and new alliance practices

---

CHAPTER 14: THE SEVEN YEARS' WAR

- Diplomatic Revolution and rearranged alliances in Europe
- Britain and Prussia vs. France, Austria, Russia; the crucial role of Frederick the Great
- Colonial theaters: North America (French and Indian War), India, and the Caribbean
- Treaty of Paris (1763) and Treaty of Hubertusburg: Britain's global ascendancy, Prussia's survival

---

CHAPTER 15: THE NAPOLEONIC WARS (PART 1)

- Napoleon's rise from the Directory coup (1799) to Emperor of the French (1804)
- Wars of the Second to Fourth Coalitions: Marengo, Austerlitz, Jena-Auerstedt, Friedland
- Napoleonic reorganization of Europe (Confederation of the Rhine, Duchy of Warsaw)
- Continental System's economic blockade and its impact

CHAPTER 16: THE NAPOLEONIC WARS (PART 2)

- The Peninsular War in Spain and Portugal: guerrilla tactics and British aid
- Austrian resurgence (1809), subsequent defeat, and Napoleon's marriage ties
- Invasion of Russia (1812), the catastrophic retreat from Moscow, and the War of the Sixth Coalition
- Leipzig's "Battle of the Nations" (1813), Napoleon's abdication, Hundred Days, and final defeat at Waterloo (1815)

CHAPTER 17: CONFLICTS IN THE 19TH CENTURY — FROM THE GREEK WAR OF INDEPENDENCE TO THE FRANCO-PRUSSIAN WAR

- Greek struggle against Ottoman rule, rise of Philhellenism, and Great Power intervention
- The Revolutions of 1848 and the failure of liberal-nationalist uprisings
- Crimean War (1853–1856) and the decline of the Concert of Europe
- Italian unification conflicts and the Franco-Prussian War (1870–1871) leading to German unification

---

CHAPTER 18: THE WARS OF THE 19TH CENTURY — COLONIAL STRUGGLES AND RISING NATIONALISM

- American Civil War (1861–1865): industrialized warfare, emancipation, and federal authority
- Opium Wars in China and the opening of East Asia to Western influence
- Scramble for Africa, Anglo-Zulu War, and other colonial campaigns
- Indian Rebellion of 1857 and the tightening of British Raj

CHAPTER 19: WORLD WAR I

- Causes: nationalism, imperial rivalries, militarism, and entangling alliances
- Sarajevo assassination and the July Crisis sparking a global conflict
- Stalemate on the Western Front, trench warfare, and huge battles
- Russia's exit and America's entry in 1917, final Allied offensives, and the Armistice of 1918
- Treaty of Versailles, collapse of empires, and unresolved tensions

---

CHAPTER 20: WORLD WAR II

- Rise of fascist regimes in Germany, Italy, and Japan, and the failure of appeasement
- Blitzkrieg campaigns, fall of France, the Battle of Britain, and Operation Barbarossa
- Pearl Harbor, the global scope of war, and major turning points
- Total war, the Holocaust, atomic bombs, and Axis defeat in 1945
- Postwar outcomes: emergence of superpowers, United Nations, and decolonization trends

Chapter 1: Early Warfare and the Dawn of Organized Armies

Introduction
Warfare has been a part of human life for thousands of years. In the simplest terms, war is a state of conflict between groups. In the distant past, small skirmishes might have involved only a handful of fighters, often with weapons made from stone or simple metals. As societies became more organized, so did their methods of combat. Once people formed communities—like towns or city-states—they felt the need to defend their lands and resources. Over time, this need sparked the growth of larger, more structured armies.

In this chapter, we will explore how warfare started, looking at the first organized armies in prehistory and early history. We will examine why people fought, how they prepared for war, and which weapons and strategies they used. This is the beginning of a story that shaped the world.

The Roots of War in Prehistory

Before written records, humans lived in small groups that roamed around looking for food. Conflict was usually small-scale and may have been limited to individual fights or short clashes over hunting grounds. Archeological evidence—like bones with injuries and ancient settlements burned to the ground—suggests that violence between groups was not uncommon. However, it was probably very different from the large-scale wars we think of today.

- **Small Groups and Clan Conflicts**
  Early humans did not have formal military ranks or training. People fought to protect themselves, their families, or their resources. They might also have fought to maintain honor, avenge a wrongdoing, or settle disputes over land. Because they traveled in small groups, they lacked the manpower and resources to create large armies. Their weapons were simple—spears, clubs, and bows made from basic materials.
- **Evidence of Organized Violence**
  Archeologists have found mass graves from the late Stone Age and early Bronze Age that indicate group violence. Sometimes these graves show

signs of repeated blows, suggesting that these people were killed in battle. Ancient wall paintings or carvings also depict scenes that look like battles. While it is hard to piece together exact events from so long ago, these clues reveal that organized violence is nearly as old as humanity itself.

The Shift Toward Settled Societies

The creation of permanent settlements was a huge turning point in human history. Once people learned to farm, they no longer needed to move around all the time. They built villages and later, small city-states. These communities began to store food and accumulate wealth in the form of crops or domesticated animals. But when a society becomes wealthy, it also becomes a target for others who want to take those resources.

- **The Rise of Agriculture**
  When people settled down to farm, they had to protect their land and food sources. This need for security led to the building of walls, fortifications, and other defensive structures. Over time, communities realized it was beneficial to have a certain group of people—often young men—focused on defense and combat. This was the start of more organized armies.
- **Trade and Interaction**
  Farming allowed societies to grow larger. More people meant more potential for conflict, but it also meant more opportunities for trade. Early settlements traded goods like pottery, metals, and textiles. However, increased interaction sometimes caused friction. Misunderstandings, competition for resources, or plain greed often resulted in conflict.

The Earliest Records of War

As soon as writing was invented, people began to record important events, including wars. The oldest known writings that mention battles come from Mesopotamia, in the region known as the Fertile Crescent (roughly modern-day

Iraq and parts of surrounding countries). Here, city-states like Uruk, Ur, and Lagash fought each other for water and farmland.

- **City-States and Their Armies**
  In Mesopotamia, each city had a ruling class that sought to increase its power. Armies were usually made up of farmers or commoners who were called to fight when needed. Commanders and scribes might take note of victories on stone tablets. Some of these inscriptions survive to this day, telling stories of conquests and treaties.
- **The Case of Sumer**
  Sumer was one of the earliest civilizations in Mesopotamia. It was divided into various city-states, each controlled by a king or high priest. These rulers often tried to expand their territory. For example, the King of Umma might lead a raid into Lagash to capture farmland. In response, Lagash would assemble its fighters to drive them back. These local wars were frequent and helped shape the region's political landscape for centuries.

Military Innovations in the Ancient Near East

As warfare became more common, people started to innovate. The invention of bronze (an alloy of copper and tin) provided a stronger metal for weapons. Bronze swords, spears, and armor replaced earlier stone or copper tools. This leap in technology allowed armies to be better equipped, and it also influenced how they fought.

- **Bronze Weapons**
  Bronze weapons lasted longer and were more effective than earlier materials. Swords became standard in some armies. Spears and axes were also improved by adding bronze tips. Though expensive to make, these weapons gave an advantage to those who could afford them, often the wealthiest city-states.
- **The Advent of the Wheel**
  The invention of the wheel, and later the chariot, was another major step. Wheeled carts and chariots made it possible to move supplies and soldiers more quickly. Armies could travel further and launch surprise

attacks on settlements that might not expect a distant foe. This also gave rise to the first real "mobile" units in warfare.
- **Fortifications and Siege Warfare**
As offensive technology improved, so did defensive methods. Cities built thicker walls, sometimes with towers to station archers. Moats or ditches might surround a settlement to slow down attackers. In response, attackers developed early forms of siege warfare, like ramming gates or digging tunnels to undermine walls.

The Emergence of Professional Soldiers

In these early societies, most men were not full-time warriors. They farmed or worked in trades and only fought when summoned. However, as wars became more frequent and territories expanded, some rulers recognized the benefit of having a permanent fighting force. This changed the nature of war.

- **Standing Armies**
A standing army is a group of soldiers who train and fight full-time. Mesopotamian kings, and later Egyptian pharaohs, began to keep a segment of their population ready to march at a moment's notice. These soldiers often received better training and equipment, making them more effective in battle.
- **Mercenaries**
Alongside standing armies, some rulers hired mercenaries. These were professional fighters who offered their services for pay. Mercenaries could come from different regions, bringing unique skills or fighting styles. However, they could be expensive, and their loyalty was always in question.

Early Moral and Cultural Aspects of War

Many of the ancient records that describe war also mention the approval of the gods or a sense of divine mandate. Rulers often claimed to be favored by a specific deity, using this as justification for conquest. War was seen as a test of a people's strength and moral right to expand. This blending of religion and warfare shaped how societies viewed their victories and defeats.

- **Gods of War**
  In Mesopotamia, the goddess Inanna (also known as Ishtar) was linked to love and war. Cities built temples to honor her, hoping to win her blessing. Similarly, Egyptians looked to gods like Montu, who was associated with war. This religious backing gave battles a sense of cosmic importance.
- **Propaganda in Stone**
  Victorious kings often erected monuments or stelae to celebrate their triumphs. These inscriptions described how they had the support of the gods or how they fought for righteous causes. Sometimes they exaggerated the scale of the enemy forces or the glory of their own army. This was an early form of propaganda, meant to legitimize the ruler's power.

Case Study: The Early Dynastic Wars of Mesopotamia

One key example of early organized warfare is found in the Early Dynastic period of Mesopotamia (around 2900–2334 BCE). City-states like Uruk, Ur, Kish, Umma, and Lagash vied for control of fertile land. Kings led campaigns to capture resources, while scribes immortalized these events on clay tablets.

- **The Stele of the Vultures**
  Perhaps the oldest known war monument is the Stele of the Vultures from the city-state of Lagash. It dates to around 2500 BCE and depicts a victory by King Eannatum of Lagash over Umma. One side of the stele shows the king leading his troops in an orderly formation. The other side shows ravens or vultures picking at the bodies of the defeated. This is one of the earliest visual records of a structured military formation.
- **Territorial Disputes**
  Most conflicts were about farmland. Because Mesopotamia's climate was harsh, controlling irrigation systems was crucial. If one city diverted a river, it could cripple another city's crops. These disputes led to a cycle of violence, where a short period of peace would follow a conquest, only to spark another war later.

Broadening Our View: Early Warfare Elsewhere

While Mesopotamia gives us some of the earliest written records, other regions also developed forms of early warfare. In the Indus Valley (in modern-day Pakistan and northwest India), archaeological evidence points to fortified cities like Mohenjo-Daro and Harappa. In China, the legendary Xia and Shang dynasties (though details are partly mythological) also engaged in battle, using bronze weapons and chariots. In Mesoamerica, early civilizations had ceremonial centers and possibly conflicts, though much is shrouded in mystery due to the lack of written records from that period.

- **Egypt**
  The unification of Upper and Lower Egypt under pharaohs like Narmer (around 3100 BCE) suggests warfare was involved in bringing these regions together. Early Egyptian armies might not have been as large as those in later kingdoms, but the concept of a unified fighting force emerged. Artwork, such as the Narmer Palette, shows battle scenes and the subjugation of enemies.
- **Early Europe**
  In parts of Europe, especially around the Mediterranean, small kingdoms and tribes often fought each other. The Bronze Age in Europe saw the spread of metal weapons, with some areas building hillforts. Although we have fewer written records, archaeology reveals a pattern of conflict over territory and resources.

The Influence of Geography

Geography played a large role in how early wars were fought. Rivers provided transport routes and fertile soil, so cities built near them often thrived. Deserts, mountains, or thick forests could act as natural barriers, making invasions more difficult. In the Fertile Crescent, flat land with few natural barriers meant armies could move relatively freely. This led to frequent clashes between city-states.

- **Climate and Strategy**
  Warfare in a desert or steppe environment might involve swift attacks and retreats, as armies had to worry about finding water. In heavily forested areas, ambushes and small raids were more common. Over time,

people adapted their tactics to the land, influencing everything from the type of weaponry used to the formation of armies.

The Significance of Early Warfare

You might wonder why these small-scale wars matter so much. They set the foundation for everything that came after. From the way armies were organized to the way fortifications were built, these early conflicts taught societies what worked and what did not. They also led to innovations in technology, governance, and even culture.

- **Centralized Authority**
  Rulers who could consistently defend or expand their territory gained more power. This led to more centralized forms of government, where a king or pharaoh held ultimate authority. Over time, this centralized power could become absolute, as in the case of Egyptian pharaohs, who were seen as living gods.
- **Spread of Ideas**
  War was also a driver for the spread of ideas. When armies traveled, they carried their culture, technology, and beliefs with them. Even in defeat, they might leave behind new practices or introduce foreign goods. This exchange could shape art, religion, language, and social structures.

Key Takeaways

1. **Warfare in Prehistory**: Long before written records, humans engaged in violent clashes, though on a smaller scale than later organized wars.
2. **Settled Societies**: The advent of farming led to permanent settlements, which became targets for raids and conquests. This pushed communities to create more formal militaries.
3. **Early Records**: Mesopotamia gives us some of the first written accounts of warfare. City-states fought for farmland and water rights, documenting victories in stone.

4. **Military Innovations**: The use of bronze for weapons, the invention of chariots, and the building of walls changed the face of war. Some leaders formed standing armies or hired mercenaries.
5. **Religious and Cultural Impact**: Many ancient wars were justified by divine will. Victories were recorded on monuments that served as both propaganda and historical record.
6. **Geographical Factors**: The layout of the land shaped strategy, affecting how armies fought and how societies defended themselves.
7. **Laying the Groundwork**: These early wars influenced later empires and kingdoms. Tactics, technology, and leadership models would continue to evolve as civilizations grew stronger.

Conclusion

In the earliest days of warfare, humans learned how to fight in groups, develop new weapons, and defend their territories with a sense of unity. These lessons paved the way for more powerful civilizations. As we move forward in history, we will see how these foundations grew into vast armies that could conquer enormous territories. The next step in our journey takes us to the rise and fall of early empires in Mesopotamia and Egypt—two regions whose power struggles left an indelible mark on the world.

Chapter 2: The Rise and Fall of Mesopotamian and Egyptian Powers

Introduction

In our first chapter, we examined how warfare developed among the earliest groups and city-states. We saw how Mesopotamia set the stage for organized armies and how societies like Egypt began to form more centralized governments. Now, we will focus on the great powers that emerged in these regions. Mesopotamia and Egypt both became centers of civilization, boasting innovations in writing, art, and government. However, each also relied heavily on the success of its military to maintain control and expand.

In this chapter, we will look closer at famous Mesopotamian empires—like the Akkadians and the Babylonians—and explore how their conquests reshaped the Middle East. We will also examine the Old, Middle, and New Kingdoms of Egypt, highlighting how the Nile River region built an impressive military machine to guard its wealth and territory. Along the way, we will discuss the factors that led to both the rise and the fall of these powers.

The Akkadian Empire: An Early Imperial Model

Historians generally regard the Akkadian Empire (c. 2334–2154 BCE) as the first real empire in history. It emerged under the leadership of Sargon of Akkad, who united many of the Sumerian city-states under one rule. The Akkadians brought innovations to warfare, statecraft, and administration, which influenced future empires.

- **Sargon of Akkad**
  Sargon's background is shrouded in legend. Some stories say he began as a cupbearer to a king before seizing power. What is clearer is that once Sargon controlled Akkad, he moved swiftly to bring neighboring cities under his rule. His military campaigns reached beyond Sumer, extending north into parts of modern-day Syria.
- **Akkadian Military Tactics**
  The Akkadians used a combination of infantry and chariotry, although their chariots were still quite primitive by later standards. They benefited

from improved bronze weapons and organized military leadership. Sargon also placed trusted officials—often his own family members—in key positions throughout the empire to maintain control.

- **Administration and Control**
  The Akkadians introduced a centralized system where taxes, tribute, and resources flowed to the capital. This helped maintain a standing army. Local rulers could keep their positions if they remained loyal to Sargon. This system, however, relied heavily on continuous military success.
- **Collapse of the Akkadian Empire**
  After Sargon's death, his descendants tried to keep the empire intact, but internal rebellions and external pressures mounted. Environmental changes, such as drought, may have worsened social and economic problems. By around 2150 BCE, the empire fell, leaving behind a power vacuum that later dynasties and empires sought to fill.

The Third Dynasty of Ur and the Neo-Sumerian Period

After the Akkadian collapse, various city-states tried to assert dominance. The Third Dynasty of Ur (Ur III) rose to prominence around 2112 BCE and revived much of the Sumerian culture. Under kings like Ur-Nammu and Shulgi, Ur III expanded its territory and tried to restore the glory that had once belonged to Sumer.

- **Ur-Nammu's Code**
  Ur-Nammu created one of the earliest known law codes. While not a direct account of warfare, these laws governed society and provided stability, which in turn supported the military. The code addressed murder, theft, and other crimes, aiming to create a well-ordered realm.
- **Military Structure**
  Ur III used a structured system of local governors who could raise troops when needed. Regular conscription and well-defined administrative records allowed the kings to mobilize resources effectively. This approach helped maintain power but also required constant vigilance.
- **Challenges and Decline**
  Despite its organization, Ur III faced threats from the Amorites in the west and the Elamites in the east. Economic strain and invasions eventually brought down the Ur III dynasty around 2004 BCE. Again, a

period of fracturing followed, where Mesopotamia lacked a single dominant power.

The Old Babylonian Empire and Hammurabi

One of the most famous rulers in Mesopotamian history is Hammurabi (c. 1792–1750 BCE), the sixth king of the First Babylonian Dynasty. He is best known for his law code, the Code of Hammurabi, which set standards of justice with the phrase "an eye for an eye." However, Hammurabi was also a skilled diplomat and warrior who expanded Babylon's territory through alliances and warfare.

- **Rise of Babylon**
  Babylon was originally a small city-state among many. Hammurabi spent years forming strategic alliances with neighboring rulers, then turned on them when it suited him. In a series of campaigns, he conquered much of Mesopotamia, making Babylon the new center of power.
- **Military and Strategy**
  Like previous empires, Babylon relied on a combination of foot soldiers and chariots. Hammurabi's real genius lay in his political strategy. He would form pacts with certain states to fight a common enemy, then once victorious, he might break those pacts if it served Babylon's interest.
- **Administration Under Hammurabi**
  The empire was divided into provinces overseen by loyal governors. Hammurabi's code helped unify these provinces under a shared legal framework. Tribute and taxes were collected systematically to support the army and fund public projects.
- **End of the Old Babylonian Empire**
  After Hammurabi's death, his successors struggled to maintain the empire against outside forces like the Hittites and Kassites. Babylon eventually lost its dominant position. Still, Hammurabi's centralized style of rule and codified laws left a lasting legacy.

Egypt's Old Kingdom and the Concept of Divine Kingship

Moving west to the Nile River Valley, ancient Egypt followed a different path but still relied on military might to unify and protect its territory. The Old Kingdom

(c. 2686–2181 BCE) is often remembered for the building of the pyramids. However, the same organizational power that built these monumental structures also supported Egypt's armies.

- **Unification of Upper and Lower Egypt**
  The unification credited to a ruler named Narmer (or Menes) laid the groundwork for Egypt's centralized government. Pharaohs were viewed not just as kings but as living gods on earth. This divine status gave them immense control over resources and labor.
- **Old Kingdom Military**
  In the Old Kingdom, Egypt's military was not as expansionist as it would become later. Armies were often raised for defense or to protect mining expeditions in the Sinai. Soldiers might also be used to quell rebellions in outlying areas. The Nile itself provided a natural defense, limiting the need for constant warfare.
- **Collapse of the Old Kingdom**
  The Old Kingdom fell due to a mixture of economic troubles, weak leadership, and possibly climatic changes that caused famine. Central authority broke down, leading to a period known as the First Intermediate Period. Local rulers (nomarchs) gained power, and the pharaoh's ability to control the entire region faded.

The Middle Kingdom: A Revival of Egyptian Power

After a time of disunity, a strong ruler from Thebes managed to reunite Egypt, ushering in the Middle Kingdom (c. 2055–1650 BCE). This era is often seen as a golden age of literature, art, and stable government. The pharaohs of the Middle Kingdom also had better-organized armies, allowing them to secure trade routes and expand Egyptian influence south into Nubia.

- **Military Campaigns**
  The Middle Kingdom pharaohs conducted military campaigns primarily to protect or gain resources. Nubia was rich in gold mines, and controlling that region was economically vital. While these campaigns were not huge compared to later Egyptian history, they helped develop more systematic approaches to waging war.

- **Fortifications in Nubia**
  The Egyptians built a series of forts along the Nile in Nubia. These forts served as defensive outposts, but they also projected power. Soldiers stationed there could respond quickly to threats and keep the Nubian population under control.
- **Second Intermediate Period**
  The Middle Kingdom eventually weakened, leading to the Second Intermediate Period. During this time, a group called the Hyksos, likely from the Levant, took control of Lower Egypt. They introduced new military technology, including the horse-drawn chariot and improved bows, which Egyptians later adopted.

The New Kingdom: Egypt as an Imperial Power

The expulsion of the Hyksos marked the start of the New Kingdom (c. 1550–1077 BCE), Egypt's most militant era. Pharaohs like Ahmose I, Thutmose III, and Ramses II built huge armies, conquered vast territories, and turned Egypt into a major power in the ancient world.

- **Ahmose I and the Rise of the New Kingdom**
  Ahmose I, the founder of the 18th Dynasty, drove out the Hyksos and reclaimed Lower Egypt. He reorganized the army, incorporating chariot units and better weapons. His success set a precedent for future expansion.
- **Thutmose III: The Napoleon of Egypt**
  Thutmose III is often called "the Napoleon of Egypt" because of his countless campaigns and strategic brilliance. He led multiple expeditions into the Levant and Syria, bringing wealth and tribute back to Thebes. His military was well-structured, with chariots, archers, and infantry working together.
- **Ramses II and the Battle of Kadesh**
  Ramses II continued the trend of military might. He fought the Hittites at the famous Battle of Kadesh (c. 1274 BCE), one of the earliest well-documented battles in history. While both sides claimed victory, the encounter led to the first recorded peace treaty. This event highlights the level of organization and diplomacy in ancient warfare.

- **Decline of the New Kingdom**
  After Ramses II, Egypt gradually lost control of its empire. Internal strife and external pressures, including invasions by the Sea Peoples, weakened the state. By the end of the New Kingdom, Egypt no longer stood as the dominant power it once was. Another period of disunity followed, known as the Third Intermediate Period.

Mesopotamia's Later Empires: Assyria and Neo-Babylon

While Egypt rose and fell, Mesopotamia continued to produce new powers. Two notable ones during the late second and early first millennium BCE were the Assyrian Empire and the Neo-Babylonian Empire.

- **The Assyrian Empire**
  The Assyrians are famous for their military prowess and harsh tactics. They were among the first to systematically use iron weapons, giving them a technological edge. Their empire, at its height (around the 7th century BCE), stretched from parts of modern-day Iran to Egypt.
    - **Military Structure**: The Assyrian army was highly organized, with specialized units of cavalry, chariots, archers, and siege engineers. They used battering rams, siege towers, and tunnels to breach city walls.
    - **Terror Tactics**: The Assyrians often used fear to suppress rebellions. They would deport entire populations, destroy cities, or display the bodies of defeated enemies. While brutal, these measures sometimes kept conquered regions in line for a time.
- **Neo-Babylonian Empire**
  After the fall of the Assyrians, the Neo-Babylonian Empire arose in the late 7th century BCE. King Nebuchadnezzar II expanded Babylonian territory and invested in monumental building projects like the Hanging Gardens (though their true existence is debated).
    - **Military Achievements**: The Neo-Babylonians captured Jerusalem, taking many Jews into captivity (the Babylonian Exile). They fortified Babylon, making it one of the most impressive cities of the ancient world.
    - **Decline**: The empire was short-lived. The Persians, under Cyrus the Great, conquered Babylon in 539 BCE. This ended the age of

independent Mesopotamian empires, as Persian rule introduced a new chapter in the region's history.

Economic and Social Factors Behind Rise and Fall

When we look at these great powers—Akkad, Babylon, Egypt—it is clear that military strength alone could not hold them together forever. Economic stability, trade routes, social cohesion, and technological edges also mattered. When these factors broke down, empires became vulnerable to outside invasion or internal collapse.

- **Resource Management**
  Armies need to be fed and paid. If a kingdom's economy fails, the military suffers. In regions like Mesopotamia, drought or changes in river flow could destroy agriculture. In Egypt, poor Nile flooding could lead to famine. Such issues could weaken a ruler's hold on power.
- **Administrative Complexity**
  Large empires require efficient administration. If local governors became too independent or corrupt, rebellions might break out. Overextension—trying to control too large a territory—could spread the army thin, making it hard to respond to uprisings or invasions.
- **Cultural Integration**
  Some empires tried to incorporate conquered peoples through shared laws, marriages, or religious practices. Others relied on intimidation or forced relocation. Over time, harsh methods could foster resentment, leading to revolts that might topple a ruling dynasty.

Technological Advancements and Warfare

Each successive empire built on earlier knowledge. The shift from bronze to iron weapons was crucial. Iron was stronger and more abundant, making it easier to equip large armies. The development of advanced siege weapons—like battering rams with iron tips—allowed armies to capture fortified cities that once seemed impenetrable.

- **Naval Warfare**
  Although less common in Mesopotamia and Egypt, naval engagements did occur, especially for riverine or Mediterranean campaigns. Egyptian reliefs sometimes show ships carrying troops or engaging in small-scale battles on the Nile.
- **Logistics and Supply**
  As empires expanded, they needed to move troops across long distances. Roads and supply depots became essential. The Assyrians built a network of roads to speed up troop movements. In Egypt, the Nile served as a natural highway, facilitating the transport of soldiers, horses, and supplies.

Cultural and Religious Aspects of Imperial Warfare

Both Mesopotamian and Egyptian kings often claimed divine support or lineage. This reinforced the idea that conquering new lands was not just a political mission but a sacred duty. Temples and priests also played a role, supporting rulers who funded them generously.

- **Mesopotamian Gods and War**
  Deities like Marduk (in Babylon) or Ashur (in Assyria) were often presented as supreme gods under whose favor the empire expanded. Kings built grand temples to honor these gods, expecting blessings for their military campaigns.
- **Egyptian Afterlife and Warfare**
  In Egypt, the pharaoh's military success was sometimes tied to maintaining Ma'at—the concept of cosmic order. Defeating foreign enemies was seen as a way to uphold this balance. Some pharaohs depicted themselves smiting enemies in temple reliefs, showing that they were fulfilling their divine role.

Lessons Learned from Ancient Empires

1. **Unity and Centralization**: Empires that managed to unify diverse peoples under a stable government often lasted longer.

2. **Technological Edge**: The adoption of better weapons and tactics could give one empire a crucial advantage.
3. **Economic Stability**: A strong agricultural base, control of trade routes, and efficient taxation were vital for sustaining large armies.
4. **Administrative Skill**: Even the strongest military cannot hold an empire together if local rulers become disloyal or resources are mismanaged.
5. **Adaptation**: Empires that adapted to new threats—like Egypt adopting the chariot after the Hyksos invasion—were more likely to survive.

Chapter 3: The Greco-Persian Struggles

Introduction

By the dawn of the fifth century BCE, two very different worlds existed on opposite shores of the Aegean Sea. To the east was the vast Persian Empire, which, under leaders such as Cyrus the Great and Darius I, had expanded across much of the Middle East. To the west lay the Greek city-states, small in territory but proud of their cultural achievements and independent spirit. Though these city-states were often at odds with each other, they shared common language, religion, and customs.

Eventually, tensions grew between the Persians, who wished to control or influence Greek cities in Asia Minor, and the mainland Greeks, who resented Persian interference. The resulting wars—commonly called the Greco-Persian Wars—lasted for several decades and became a defining moment in Western history. The outcome would shape the trajectory of Greek civilization, influencing not just military tactics but also politics, art, and self-identity. In this chapter, we will explore how these struggles began, the key battles, the leading figures, and how victory or defeat reshaped the ancient world.

Background: The Rise of Persia and Early Friction

Persia Before the Wars

The Persian Empire began as a small kingdom in southwestern Iran. Under Cyrus the Great (r. 559–530 BCE), Persia expanded at a tremendous pace, conquering the Medes and then moving westward to take over Lydia and Babylon. After Cyrus died, his successors, Cambyses II and especially Darius I, continued to grow Persian power. By the time of Darius, the empire stretched from parts of Central Asia all the way to Egypt and the eastern edge of the Aegean Sea.

To manage this enormous realm, the Persians developed efficient administrative systems, including a network of roads and regional governors known as satraps. Their approach to conquered peoples was often pragmatic; they allowed local customs and religions to continue as long as taxes were paid and loyalty was maintained. However, certain regions proved less easy to govern, and tensions sometimes flared.

The Ionian Revolt

One significant spark of conflict between Persia and the Greek world was the Ionian Revolt (499–493 BCE). The Ionian Greeks lived in coastal cities on the western edge of Asia Minor (modern-day Turkey). They had long been under the rule of the Lydians and, after Lydia fell to Persia, under Persian authority. Though Persia allowed some local autonomy, many Ionian Greeks felt burdened by heavy taxes and resented Persian-appointed tyrants who ruled their cities.

In 499 BCE, a revolt broke out when Aristagoras, the tyrant of Miletus, failed in a Persian-backed campaign and feared losing his power. He stirred up resentment among his fellow Ionians, and several cities rose in rebellion. The Ionian rebels appealed to mainland Greece for help. Athens and Eretria sent ships and some troops. This Athenian assistance, though modest, was significant because it directly challenged Persian authority.

The Ionian Revolt lasted about six years. At first, the rebels managed some victories, even burning the regional Persian capital of Sardis. Eventually, the Persians—better organized and far more numerous—crushed the revolt. Miletus, a leading Ionian city, was sacked, and its people were either killed or sold into slavery. The rebellion failed, but it sowed seeds of animosity. Darius, enraged by the role Athens played, turned his attention to the Greek mainland. According to some accounts, he reportedly had a servant remind him daily to "remember the Athenians," a reflection of his desire for revenge.

First Persian Invasion (492–490 BCE)

Darius' Preparations

After quelling the Ionian Revolt, Darius prepared for a punitive expedition against Athens. He wanted to punish the Athenians and Eretrians for aiding the revolt and possibly bring all of Greece under Persian dominion. In 492 BCE, he sent a force under his son-in-law, Mardonius, to subdue Thrace and Macedonia, aiming to secure a base closer to mainland Greece. Although this campaign partially succeeded, storms destroyed much of the Persian fleet off the coast. Mardonius had to retreat, delaying the invasion.

The Attack on Eretria

Two years later, Darius tried again. This time, he dispatched an expedition led by Datis and Artaphernes. The Persian army crossed the Aegean, capturing islands along the way. Eretria, on the island of Euboea, was besieged and fell after some internal treachery. The city was burned, and its people were taken as prisoners.

The Battle of Marathon

With Eretria subdued, the Persians moved on to Attica, planning to punish Athens. They landed their forces on the Marathon plain, about 25 miles from Athens. The Athenian army, outnumbered (modern historians still debate the figures, but traditional accounts say around 10,000 Athenians against 25,000 Persians), took a bold step. Rather than waiting inside city walls, the Athenian generals—especially Miltiades—chose to meet the Persians on the battlefield.

In a surprising tactical move, the Athenians strengthened their wings and attacked swiftly, encircling the Persian center. The Persians, unprepared for the Greek style of close-quarters hoplite combat, broke ranks. Many ran back to their ships; some drowned in the marshes behind the battlefield. The victory at Marathon was astounding for the Athenians. They lost fewer than 200 men according to ancient sources, while Persian casualties numbered in the thousands.

The Battle of Marathon became legendary. It showed that the Persian army, though large, was not invincible. It also boosted Athenian confidence and pride. The story of a runner named Pheidippides, who raced from the battlefield back to Athens to announce victory (and supposedly died upon delivering the message), became a symbol of endurance and sacrifice. Though the details are debated by historians, the core message—that Athens had withstood the might of Persia—remained a cornerstone in the city's lore.

Second Persian Invasion (480–479 BCE)

Xerxes Takes Command

After the failure at Marathon, Darius planned a larger invasion, but he died before seeing it through. His son Xerxes inherited the throne and vowed to avenge his father's defeat. Xerxes spent several years mustering a massive force, drawing troops from all corners of the Persian Empire. Estimates of the size of this army vary wildly in ancient sources—from a few hundred thousand to over two million. Modern scholars generally assume the force was very large but not as enormous as ancient Greek writers claimed.

Xerxes also ordered the construction of a bridge (a boat-bridge) across the Hellespont (the strait now known as the Dardanelles) to move his army from Asia into Europe. This ambitious engineering project showcased Persian logistical prowess.

Greek Preparations and Alliances

Meanwhile, the Greek city-states realized they would need to unite or face certain conquest. Though these city-states were often hostile to each other, the looming Persian threat forced cooperation. Athens put its resources into building a more powerful navy, influenced by the leader Themistocles, who convinced the Athenians to use newly discovered silver mines to fund shipbuilding.

A council of Greek states formed, with Sparta recognized as the leader on land and Athens acknowledged as the strongest naval power. Many smaller poleis (Greek city-states) either joined this alliance or tried to remain neutral, hoping to avoid destruction.

The Battle of Thermopylae

Xerxes set forth in 480 BCE, leading an immense army by land while a large fleet sailed along the coast. The Greeks decided to make their stand at Thermopylae, a narrow pass in northern Greece. A small force, led by the Spartan King Leonidas, held the pass to delay the Persians and buy time for the rest of Greece to prepare. According to tradition, Leonidas commanded about 300 Spartans, supported by a few thousand allies.

For two days, the Persian army was held at bay. The narrow terrain negated their numbers, and the Greek hoplites' discipline proved effective. On the third day, a local named Ephialtes showed Xerxes a secret mountain path that allowed Persian troops to flank the defenders. Surrounded, Leonidas and his men fought to the death, refusing to retreat. While Thermopylae was ultimately a Persian victory, it became a symbol of courage and sacrifice for the Greeks. The delay allowed the other city-states more time to organize defenses.

Naval Action at Artemisium

Simultaneously, the Greek navy tried to block the Persian fleet at the strait of Artemisium, near the island of Euboea. Fights broke out over several days, with heavy losses on both sides. When news of the defeat at Thermopylae reached the Greek fleet, they decided to withdraw to Salamis rather than risk being trapped.

The Sack of Athens

With the land route now open, Xerxes' army marched south. Many Greek states had submitted to him. Athens, having evacuated its citizens to nearby islands, was left nearly empty. The Persians entered Athens and burned the city, including the old temples on the Acropolis. While a huge morale blow, the Athenian fleet still remained intact, and the war was far from over.

The Battle of Salamis

Faced with the destruction of Athens, Themistocles pressed the Greek fleet—made up of triremes from various city-states—to take a stand at the narrow waters off Salamis. Xerxes, confident in his numbers, wanted to finish the war swiftly, so he sent his ships into the straits.

The narrow passages at Salamis favored the smaller Greek fleet. Persian ships, caught in cramped waters, struggled to maneuver. The heavier Greek triremes crashed into the Persian vessels, sinking many. Xerxes, watching from a throne on the shore, was horrified to see his armada routed. This decisive naval victory forced Xerxes to retreat with much of his army, leaving a general named Mardonius in Greece to continue the fight.

The Battle of Plataea

In the spring of 479 BCE, the Greeks assembled a large army under Spartan command to confront Mardonius near Plataea in Boeotia. The battle was fiercely contested, but the Greek hoplites again proved superior. Mardonius was killed, and his forces scattered. On roughly the same day, a Greek fleet triumphed at Mycale in Ionia, destroying the remnants of the Persian navy beached along the coast. These twin victories ended the main Persian threat on land and sea.

Aftermath and Significance

The Greek victory in the Persian Wars had huge ramifications:

1. **Preservation of Greek Independence**: Had Persia conquered all of Greece, the cultural and political life of the city-states might have been crushed or altered. Democracy, especially in Athens, could have been suppressed.
2. **Rise of Athens**: Athens emerged as a major power, especially at sea. They formed the Delian League, an alliance of Greek city-states, to continue fighting the Persians in the Aegean and Ionia. Over time, this league evolved into an Athenian empire, sparking tensions with other states like Sparta.
3. **Cultural Flowering**: The sense of pride and freedom after defeating the Persians contributed to an outpouring of art, drama, philosophy, and architecture, often associated with the "Golden Age of Athens."
4. **Shift in Warfare**: The Persian Wars highlighted the power of disciplined, heavily armed infantry (Greek hoplites) in certain terrains. It also underscored the growing importance of naval strength, as seen at Salamis.
5. **Legend and Memory**: Thermopylae, Marathon, and Salamis passed into legend, becoming enduring symbols of courage and strategic brilliance.

Key Figures

- **Darius I**: Persian Emperor who first sought to punish Athens for aiding the Ionian Revolt.

- **Xerxes**: Darius' son, who led the second, massive invasion of Greece.
- **Miltiades**: Athenian general, the architect of the victory at Marathon.
- **Leonidas**: Spartan king who led the heroic stand at Thermopylae.
- **Themistocles**: Athenian politician and general who pushed for a strong navy and devised the victory at Salamis.

Lessons from the Greco-Persian Wars

1. **Unity in the Face of a Common Foe**: The Greek city-states overcame their rivalries to stand against Persia. This unity was not perfect, but it proved enough to secure victory.
2. **Strategic Use of Terrain**: Battles at Thermopylae and Salamis show how narrower terrain can help a smaller force offset the numerical advantage of a bigger army.
3. **Naval Power**: Control of the sea can be decisive. By preventing Persian reinforcements and supplies, the Greek navy played a vital role in the war.
4. **Morale and Identity**: The Greek victory fueled a strong cultural identity, which shaped future conflicts and alliances in the ancient world.

Chapter 4: The Wars of Alexander the Great and the Hellenistic World

Introduction

After the Persian Wars, Athens and Sparta emerged as leading powers in the Greek world. Yet, constant warfare—most notably the Peloponnesian War (431–404 BCE)—drained the strength of these city-states. A new force rose to the north: Macedonia. Under King Philip II, the Macedonians transformed from a relatively marginal kingdom into a powerful military state. Then, Philip's son Alexander took the throne and achieved what many thought impossible: the complete conquest of the Persian Empire and more.

In this chapter, we will delve into the wars of Alexander the Great. We will explore how he inherited his father's formidable army, the major battles he fought against the Persian kings, his sweeping advance into Egypt and Asia, and the eventual fragmentation of his empire after his death. This period changed the cultural landscape of the eastern Mediterranean, blending Greek and local traditions in what we call the Hellenistic world.

Macedonia on the Rise

King Philip II's Military Reforms

Philip II (r. 359–336 BCE) inherited a kingdom in disarray. Surrounded by hostile neighbors—Illyrians, Thracians, and fractious Greek city-states—Macedonia needed a strong military to survive. Philip introduced key reforms:

1. **The Macedonian Phalanx**: Traditional Greek hoplites used shorter spears, around 8 feet long. Philip armed his soldiers with the sarissa, a pike nearly 18 feet in length. This allowed Macedonian infantry to strike enemy forces before they could close the distance.
2. **Professional Standing Army**: Unlike many Greek city-states that relied on citizen-soldiers, Philip created a year-round force with regular drills and standardized equipment. Soldiers became experts in coordinated maneuvers.

3. **Combined Arms**: Philip combined the heavy infantry phalanx with cavalry, archers, and specialized troops, ensuring flexibility on the battlefield. The Companion Cavalry, in particular, gained fame for its decisive charges.
4. **Diplomacy and Marriage Alliances**: Philip also formed alliances through marriage, forging connections with powerful neighbors. This reduced the number of enemies he faced at any given time.

By the mid-330s BCE, Philip had subjugated or allied with most of the Greek city-states, forming the League of Corinth. His declared goal was to lead a pan-Hellenic army against Persia, avenging the invasions of Darius and Xerxes from a century earlier. Before he could launch this grand campaign, Philip was assassinated in 336 BCE. His young son, Alexander, succeeded him.

Alexander Takes Command

Early Challenges

When Alexander became king at the age of 20, many in Greece and abroad doubted his ability. Rival factions within Macedonia tested his rule, and Greek city-states that resented Macedonian hegemony saw an opportunity to break free. However, Alexander acted decisively:

- **Elimination of Rivals**: Alexander quickly removed any threats to his throne by dealing with conspirators in the Macedonian court.
- **Speedy Suppression of Revolts**: The city of Thebes rose in rebellion. Alexander crushed it, destroying much of the city and selling its population into slavery. This severe action sent a clear message to other potential rebels: defy Alexander at your peril.

With his home front secure, Alexander turned his attention to Persia. He decided to fulfill his father's plan and lead the Greeks in a campaign of conquest.

The Persian Campaign: Breaking the Achaemenid Empire

The Crossing into Asia Minor

In 334 BCE, Alexander led an army of about 30,000 infantry and 5,000 cavalry across the Hellespont into Asia Minor (modern Turkey). Before moving further inland, he visited the site of Troy, a symbolic gesture linking his own expedition to the legendary Trojan War heroes. His force was relatively small compared to the full might of Persia, but it was disciplined, well-led, and confident.

The Battle of the Granicus (334 BCE)

Alexander's first major test came at the Granicus River, where Persian satraps gathered local forces to oppose him. Alexander charged across the river at the head of his Companion Cavalry, risking his life in the process. Despite fierce resistance, the Persian line broke under the well-coordinated attack of cavalry and the Macedonian phalanx. This victory opened Asia Minor to Alexander. Many Greek cities under Persian control welcomed him as a liberator.

Siege of Halicarnassus

Some Persian strongholds resisted, notably Halicarnassus on the southwestern coast. Alexander employed siege engines, sappers, and continuous assaults. The defenders eventually fled by sea, leaving the city to Alexander's troops. His success in siege warfare showed that the Macedonians could tackle fortified positions as well as open-field battles.

From Asia Minor to Phoenicia and Egypt

The Battle of Issus (333 BCE)

Continuing eastward, Alexander faced the main Persian force under King Darius III near the town of Issus, in southeastern Asia Minor. Despite being outnumbered, Alexander again used the combined tactics of cavalry on the flanks and the unstoppable phalanx in the center. Darius, seeing the tide turning, fled the field, leaving his family and treasury behind. The battle was a major psychological blow to Persia and a huge boost for Alexander's reputation.

The Siege of Tyre (332 BCE)

Alexander then moved into Phoenicia, where the city of Tyre refused to surrender. Tyre was located on an island, heavily fortified and protected by a formidable navy. Alexander built a causeway from the mainland to the island, using rubble and timber. His engineers devised siege towers and massive battering rams. After months of bitter struggle, the Macedonians stormed Tyre. The victory was costly, but it freed Alexander's naval flank and opened the door to Egypt.

Egypt and the Founding of Alexandria

In late 332 BCE, Alexander marched into Egypt, where he was welcomed as a liberator from Persian rule. The Egyptians crowned him as Pharaoh, and Alexander showed respect for local customs and religion. He founded the city of Alexandria on the Mediterranean coast, envisioning it as a hub of Greek culture and trade. Alexandria would later become one of the most important cities in the Hellenistic world.

The Decisive Confrontation: Gaugamela (331 BCE)

After securing Egypt, Alexander moved northeast to confront Darius III once more. The Persian king gathered an enormous army near the village of Gaugamela, not far from the ruins of Nineveh in Mesopotamia. Darius chose this battlefield carefully, ensuring flat terrain for his chariots and cavalry.

Pre-Battle Tactics

Alexander's scouts gathered information about the Persian dispositions. The night before the fight, Darius kept his army standing, fearing a surprise attack. Alexander allowed his men to rest, confident in the discipline they had shown in past victories.

Battle Dynamics

When the battle commenced, the Persians launched chariot assaults. Macedonian light infantry opened gaps in their lines to let the chariots pass, then struck the drivers. Meanwhile, Alexander led a wedge formation on the right flank, seeking to create a gap between Persian infantry and cavalry. As Darius' troops responded, Alexander found the opening he needed and charged toward the Persian center.

Darius, once again, lost his nerve and fled. With the Persian king gone, much of his army disintegrated. The victory at Gaugamela effectively ended the Achaemenid Empire. Babylon, Susa, and Persepolis soon fell to Alexander without major resistance. In a symbolic act, Alexander took control of Persepolis, the ceremonial capital, where some of his troops burned parts of the city—though the exact reasons are debated (revenge for the burning of Athens or a drunken miscalculation).

Expanding the Empire to the Edges of the Known World

The Pursuit of Darius III

Alexander chased Darius into the eastern provinces, hoping to capture him and gain legitimacy as the new Great King. Darius was murdered by one of his own satraps, Bessus, who then declared himself king. Alexander pursued Bessus into Central Asia, eventually capturing and executing him. Though the Persian throne was vacant, Alexander used the symbolism of Darius' downfall to claim he was now the rightful ruler of Persia.

The Campaign in Central Asia

The next few years saw Alexander marching through what is now Afghanistan and parts of Central Asia. He faced guerrilla warfare in mountainous regions, requiring him to found new cities and garrisons to secure his supply lines. These campaigns were tough and tested the loyalty of his troops, who had marched thousands of miles from home.

Into India: The Battle of the Hydaspes (326 BCE)

Ever ambitious, Alexander pressed on into the Indian subcontinent (modern-day Pakistan). He encountered King Porus, who commanded an army that included war elephants. At the Hydaspes River, Alexander's forces crossed secretly during a storm to surprise Porus. The elephants caused initial panic, but disciplined Macedonian units managed to isolate and attack them. Porus was eventually defeated.

Impressed by the bravery and stature of Porus, Alexander allowed him to remain a local ruler under Macedonian authority. However, the Macedonian troops, exhausted and wary of further unknown lands, refused to march deeper into India. Alexander, though disappointed, agreed to turn back.

Return and the Death of Alexander

Alexander's journey back took him along the harsh Makran coast (in modern Pakistan and Iran), where his army suffered from lack of supplies and extreme heat. Once he reached Susa and Babylon, he began plans to consolidate and govern his massive empire. He encouraged marriages between Macedonian officers and Persian noblewomen to blend the cultures, an unpopular move among many of his Macedonian core who disdained mixing with "barbarians."

In 323 BCE, at the age of 32, Alexander fell ill in Babylon and died. The exact cause of his death remains unknown—speculations range from malaria to typhoid, or possibly poisoning. With no clear heir (his son Alexander IV was an infant), the empire fragmented almost immediately, as Alexander's generals—later known as the Diadochi—fought among themselves for dominance.

The Hellenistic World After Alexander

Division of the Empire

The Diadochi carved out kingdoms:

- **Ptolemy** gained control of Egypt, founding the Ptolemaic Dynasty, which lasted until the Roman conquest under Cleopatra VII's reign centuries later.
- **Seleucus** took over much of the Asian territories, establishing the Seleucid Empire.
- **Antigonus** and later his descendants ruled parts of Asia Minor and the eastern Aegean.
- **Lysimachus** governed Thrace and parts of western Asia Minor.
- **Cassander** eventually took Macedonia and Greece.

These successor states often battled each other, but they also ushered in a period of cultural fusion. Greek influence mixed with local traditions, leading to advances in science, mathematics, art, and philosophy.

Cultural Fusion

The spread of Greek language and ideas across the Middle East and parts of Asia is one of Alexander's most enduring legacies. Greek became the lingua franca in many regions, aiding trade and intellectual exchange. Centers like Alexandria in Egypt became hubs of learning, famous for their libraries and scholars.

At the same time, local cultures did not simply vanish; they adapted and integrated Greek elements. We see Greek-style statues of Indian deities in the region of Gandhara, while in the Seleucid territories, Greek colonists absorbed aspects of Babylonian and Persian religion.

Military and Political Significance

1. **End of the Achaemenid Empire**: Alexander's campaigns permanently ended Persian rule in many areas, although new Persian-influenced states (like the Parthian Empire) would rise later.

2. **Innovation in Warfare**: The Macedonian system of combined arms and the long sarissa spear changed how battles were fought. The success of flanking maneuvers and cavalry charges influenced tactics for centuries.
3. **Foundation of Hellenistic States**: After Alexander's death, the Greek world was no longer confined to the Aegean. Instead, it stretched from Egypt to parts of India. Although politically fractured, these regions shared a Greek-influenced cultural sphere.
4. **Shift in Power Centers**: Cities like Alexandria, Antioch, and Pergamon gained prominence, reflecting the broader geography of the Hellenistic era.
5. **Integration Strategies**: Alexander's attempts to integrate Persians into his army and government were groundbreaking for the era. While not entirely successful, it foreshadowed later empires that tried to manage multi-ethnic populations.

Key Battles and Events

- **Granicus (334 BCE)**: Alexander's first victory in Asia Minor, opening the door to further conquests.
- **Issus (333 BCE)**: Darius III's defeat and flight; a major psychological triumph for Alexander.
- **Siege of Tyre (332 BCE)**: Demonstrated Alexander's skill in siege warfare and secured naval dominance.
- **Gaugamela (331 BCE)**: The decisive battle that broke the backbone of the Persian Empire.
- **Hydaspes (326 BCE)**: Victory in India against war elephants, but the limit of Alexander's eastward expansion.

Reasons for Alexander's Success

1. **Inherited Reforms**: Alexander built on Philip II's well-trained and disciplined army.
2. **Personal Leadership**: Alexander fought at the front, inspiring loyalty and respect.

3. **Flexible Strategy**: A mix of swift cavalry strikes and steady phalanx power outmatched most enemies.
4. **Divide and Conquer**: He tackled Persian forces in parts, never allowing them to unite fully under strong leadership.
5. **Adaptability**: From siege warfare to pitched battles in foreign landscapes, Alexander's forces adjusted tactics quickly.

The Downside of Unchecked Conquest

Despite his remarkable achievements, Alexander's empire was unstable from the start. Each region had its own traditions, and Alexander's attempts to unify them often sparked resentment. His Macedonian officers grumbled about adopting Persian customs, while local populations saw Macedonian garrisons as occupiers. The sheer scale of his domain made governance challenging. Alexander's early death meant there was no matured system to hold the empire together, and the Diadochi's wars shattered any hope of a unified realm.

Long-Term Legacy of the Hellenistic Period

The Hellenistic period (roughly 323–31 BCE) was marked by artistic, scientific, and philosophical achievements. Scholars like Euclid (mathematics) and Archimedes (engineering) thrived, while the Library of Alexandria stood as a beacon of learning. Greek drama, sculpture, and architecture merged with local styles, creating a rich tapestry of cultural expression.

Politically, the successor states continued to wage wars over territory, forging complex alliances or rivalries. The Ptolemies in Egypt became wealthy from trade and agriculture, turning Alexandria into a cosmopolitan center. The Seleucid Empire tried to maintain vast lands in Asia but struggled with revolts and the rise of new powers like the Parthians. Over time, Rome gradually became the arbiter of disputes in the Greek world, eventually absorbing these kingdoms one by one.

Chapter 5: The Punic Wars

Introduction

The Punic Wars were a series of three conflicts fought between Rome and Carthage from the middle of the third century BCE to the middle of the second century BCE. These wars became pivotal in shaping the future of the ancient Mediterranean world. Before the Punic Wars, Rome was a strong regional power in the Italian peninsula, while Carthage was the dominant naval power in the western Mediterranean. Over roughly a century, these two states clashed on land and sea, resulting in immense destruction—especially for Carthage—and a massive shift in regional power dynamics.

In this chapter, we will examine how Carthage and Rome became rivals, the causes and outcomes of each of the three Punic Wars, and the long-term consequences for both powers. The lessons from the Punic Wars extend beyond mere warfare; they also reveal how political structures, leadership, and strategic decisions can shape the trajectory of entire civilizations.

Setting the Stage: Rome and Carthage Before the Wars

Rome: From City-State to Regional Power

By the mid-3rd century BCE, Rome had grown from a small city-state on the Tiber River into the dominant force throughout the Italian peninsula. The Romans had battled numerous neighbors, including the Samnites, Etruscans, and various Gallic tribes, gradually consolidating power. Their political structure—an alliance system that allowed conquered peoples limited autonomy but demanded loyalty and manpower—resulted in a steady supply of soldiers. This meant Rome could field large armies for extended periods, which was crucial in lengthy conflicts.

Culturally, Roman society emphasized discipline, duty, and the importance of military service. Elite families vied for honors through military commands and political posts in the Senate. Over time, Rome's success in Italy bolstered both its confidence and its ability to expand further.

Carthage: The Naval Superpower

Carthage began as a Phoenician colony located in what is now Tunisia in North Africa. By the third century BCE, it had grown into a wealthy maritime empire with trading routes stretching across the Mediterranean. Carthaginian power rested on its navy and extensive commercial networks. The Carthaginians established colonies or trading outposts in places like Sicily, Sardinia, Corsica, and parts of southern Spain, exploiting resources and maintaining trade monopolies.

Carthage's government was somewhat oligarchic, with powerful merchant families heavily influencing policy. Unlike Rome, which relied on citizens for its core armies, Carthage often employed mercenaries—hired soldiers from various regions, including North Africa (Numidians), Iberia (modern-day Spain), and Gaul. This provided Carthage with diverse troops, but it also meant the loyalty of these forces sometimes hinged on pay and success, rather than a sense of civic duty.

Rising Tensions

Sicily emerged as the initial flashpoint for Rome and Carthage. The island was strategically important and economically valuable due to its fertile land and position between Africa and Italy. Both powers had commercial and political interests in the region, and local disputes in Sicily often pulled Carthage and Rome into the same orbit. Soon, friction over spheres of influence escalated into open hostilities.

The First Punic War (264–241 BCE)

Causes and Early Maneuvers

The First Punic War began as a conflict over the city of Messana (present-day Messina) in northeastern Sicily. A group of mercenaries called the Mamertines seized control of the city and, under threat from the nearby Greek city of Syracuse, asked for Roman help. Carthage also had an interest in the region and sent support. When the Mamertines switched their allegiance to Rome, tensions with Carthage turned into a direct confrontation.

Rome had never fought a major naval power before. Carthage, with its experienced navy, seemed likely to dominate the seas. Initially, the Romans struggled to match Carthage at sea, but they quickly adapted, building a fleet and developing innovations like the corvus, a boarding device with a spike that allowed Roman soldiers to board enemy ships and fight hand-to-hand—an approach more in line with Roman infantry tactics than traditional naval warfare.

Key Battles on Land and Sea

1. **Battle of Mylae (260 BCE)**
   This was Rome's first major naval victory. Using the corvus, the Romans turned a sea engagement into something resembling a land battle. Carthaginian ships, though maneuverable, were overwhelmed by Roman legionaries boarding them. This success boosted Roman morale and showcased their ability to learn fast.
2. **Invasion of North Africa**
   Encouraged by early naval successes, Rome attempted to strike at the heart of Carthaginian power by landing an army in North Africa around 256 BCE under the command of Marcus Atilius Regulus. Initially, the campaign went well, but the Roman forces were eventually defeated by Carthaginian armies bolstered by Greek mercenary commander Xanthippus. Many Romans were taken prisoner or killed, and the survivors fled. This setback reminded Rome that Carthage was still formidable on home soil.
3. **Continued Stalemate in Sicily**
   For many years, both sides fought back and forth in Sicily. Cities changed hands multiple times, leading to the devastation of farmlands and local populations. Siege warfare dominated much of the conflict on the island, with neither side able to completely oust the other.
4. **Naval Wars and Heavy Losses**
   Rome built multiple fleets over the course of the war, but storms and naval battles caused catastrophic losses. Carthage also suffered significant ship losses. Despite the setbacks, Rome persisted, replacing sunken fleets again and again—a testament to its large resource base and alliances within Italy.

Conclusion of the First Punic War

By 241 BCE, Carthage was worn down financially and militarily. Its mercenary-based armies were expensive to maintain, and political divisions at home complicated the war effort. Rome won a crucial naval battle off the Aegates Islands, which forced Carthage to sue for peace. Under the terms of the treaty, Carthage had to:

- Evacuate Sicily and cede it to Rome
- Pay a significant war indemnity over ten years

Rome annexed Sicily as its first overseas province, marking a major shift in Roman policy from controlling the Italian peninsula to governing territories abroad. This victory established Rome as a naval as well as a land power.

The Interwar Period and Carthaginian Resurgence

Mercenary War in Carthage

Shortly after the First Punic War, Carthage faced a crisis at home. The mercenaries, who had fought for Carthage during the war, demanded payment. Due to strained finances and possibly mismanagement, Carthage delayed or reduced their pay. This erupted into a brutal conflict known as the Mercenary War (240–238 BCE). Eventually, Carthage prevailed, but the rebellion revealed deep structural weaknesses and drained resources further.

During this turmoil, Rome took advantage of Carthage's vulnerability, occupying Sardinia and Corsica. Although these islands had been loosely tied to Carthage, the treaty's terms were interpreted by Rome in such a way as to justify annexation. The bitterness from this Roman action fueled Carthaginian resentment and set the stage for another major clash.

Hamilcar Barca and Iberian Expansion

Hamilcar Barca, a skilled Carthaginian general (and father to the future general Hannibal), sought to rebuild Carthage's fortunes by expanding into the Iberian Peninsula (modern Spain and Portugal). Rich in silver mines and other resources, Iberia promised wealth that could pay off war debts, finance new armies, and compensate for the loss of Sicily, Sardinia, and Corsica.

Hamilcar's campaigns in Iberia laid the groundwork for a revival of Carthaginian power. He secured territory, built alliances with local tribes, and eventually, Carthage controlled large parts of southeastern Iberia. When Hamilcar died, his son-in-law Hasdrubal took over, and after Hasdrubal's death, Hannibal—Hamilcar's young son—rose to command.

The Second Punic War (218–201 BCE)

Hannibal's Oath and Early Moves

Legend says Hannibal, as a boy, swore an oath to his father never to befriend Rome. True or not, Hannibal certainly carried a deep hostility toward Rome. By the time he was in command in Iberia, tensions with Rome were escalating again. Rome had a treaty with Carthage that fixed the Ebro River as the boundary in Iberia: Carthage would not expand north of the Ebro, and Rome would not interfere south of it. However, the city of Saguntum, an ally of Rome, lay south of the river. When Hannibal attacked Saguntum in 219 BCE, he effectively challenged Rome's claim.

Rome demanded Carthage hand over Hannibal; when Carthage refused, war was declared. Thus began one of history's most famous conflicts, centered on Hannibal's daring strategies, including the legendary march across the Alps.

The Crossing of the Alps

Hannibal gathered an army composed of Carthaginians, Iberian tribesmen, Numidian cavalry, and war elephants. In 218 BCE, he marched from Iberia across the Pyrenees, through southern Gaul (modern France), and then over the Alps into northern Italy. The journey was perilous: harsh weather, narrow mountain passes, and hostile tribes caused severe losses. Some ancient sources claim he started with around 40,000 infantry, 8,000 cavalry, and a few dozen elephants; by the time he reached the Italian peninsula, many had perished.

Despite these hardships, Hannibal's arrival in Italy was a massive shock to the Romans, who expected to confront him in Iberia or at sea. Hannibal's bold strategy showed that Carthage could take the war to Rome's doorstep, and it disrupted Roman plans to wage a safe, distant campaign.

Major Battles in Italy

1. **Battle of Trebia (218 BCE)**
   Soon after entering Italy, Hannibal defeated a Roman force at the Trebia River. He used a combination of ambush and superior cavalry tactics, luring the Romans into a trap where hidden Carthaginian troops attacked from the rear.
2. **Battle of Lake Trasimene (217 BCE)**
   Hannibal continued south, staging a brilliant ambush near the misty shores of Lake Trasimene. By hiding his main force in the hills around a narrow defile, he caught the Roman army off-guard. Thousands of Romans were killed or captured, and Rome realized that Hannibal's cunning far exceeded their initial expectations.
3. **Battle of Cannae (216 BCE)**
   This is perhaps Hannibal's most celebrated victory. Facing a much larger Roman force—some estimates suggest around 80,000 Romans to Hannibal's 50,000—Hannibal arranged his troops in a crescent shape with weaker units in the center and stronger infantry on the flanks. As the Romans advanced, the Carthaginian center bent back, forming a pocket. Once fully engaged, Carthaginian cavalry routed the Roman cavalry on the wings, then attacked the Roman rear. The Romans found themselves encircled, leading to an unprecedented slaughter. Possibly 50,000–70,000 Romans died that day, shaking the republic to its core.

The Roman Response and Fabian Tactics

After Cannae, many thought Rome was finished. Some southern Italian cities defected to Hannibal, hoping to be spared. Yet Rome refused to negotiate peace. Instead, it rallied new armies and adopted the so-called Fabian strategy, named after the dictator Quintus Fabius Maximus. The idea was to avoid large-scale direct battles with Hannibal, who was a master tactician, and instead harass his forces, cut off his supplies, and slowly wear him down.

This approach frustrated Hannibal because he thrived on decisive engagements. Without a major battle, he could not deliver a final knockout blow. Over time, the Romans regained control of rebellious cities and confined Hannibal's troops mostly to southern Italy.

The War Spreads: Iberia and North Africa

While Hannibal remained in Italy, Rome opened other fronts:

- **Iberia**: Roman commanders, including the Scipio family, campaigned against Carthaginian forces, aiming to cut off Hannibal's base of resources. After initial Roman setbacks, Publius Cornelius Scipio (later called Scipio Africanus) took charge, capturing Carthaginian strongholds and winning local allies.
- **Invasion of Africa**: Recognizing that Hannibal was dependent on Carthaginian support from afar, Scipio Africanus planned to strike North Africa. In 204 BCE, he landed near Utica, gaining the support of Numidian Prince Masinissa. Numidian cavalry would prove critical in later battles.

The Battle of Zama (202 BCE)

Faced with the threat to Carthage itself, the Carthaginian leadership recalled Hannibal from Italy after more than 15 years on the peninsula. Hannibal returned to Africa to defend his homeland, meeting Scipio in a decisive showdown at Zama in 202 BCE. By this time, Roman and allied cavalry had improved, and Hannibal's elephants, once a symbol of Carthaginian might, were less effective against Scipio's prepared tactics. The Roman-led forces routed Hannibal's army, forcing Carthage to negotiate peace.

Treaty Terms and Aftermath

The treaty ending the Second Punic War was harsh for Carthage:

- They had to surrender their overseas empire, effectively giving up Iberia.
- Their navy was reduced significantly, leaving Carthage unable to challenge Rome at sea.
- They had to pay a large indemnity over 50 years.
- They needed Rome's permission to engage in future wars, even for self-defense.

Carthage was not destroyed, but it was severely weakened. Rome emerged from the Second Punic War as the dominant power in the western Mediterranean, its prestige and territorial holdings vastly expanded.

The Third Punic War (149–146 BCE)

Renewed Tensions

After the Second Punic War, Carthage struggled to rebuild its economy under these strict terms. One factor that led to renewed conflict was the role of Numidia. King Masinissa, Rome's ally, frequently encroached on Carthaginian territory. Carthage, restricted by the treaty and fearful of angering Rome, tried to appeal to the Roman Senate. The Senate often sided with Masinissa or was indifferent, seeing Carthage's complaints as an annoyance.

Over time, Roman hawks—led by figures like Cato the Elder—pushed the idea that Carthage was still a threat. Cato famously ended his speeches with the phrase "Carthago delenda est" ("Carthage must be destroyed"). When Carthage eventually fought back against Numidian raids without Roman permission, Rome used this as a pretext for war.

The Siege of Carthage

In 149 BCE, Roman forces landed in North Africa, launching the Third Punic War. Carthage offered concessions, including giving up hostages, weapons, and war machines. However, Rome demanded the complete destruction of the city and relocation of its population inland. This was too much for the Carthaginians to bear, and they chose to resist.

For three years, Carthage withstood a siege, displaying remarkable resilience. The city's defenders crafted makeshift weapons and repurposed every scrap of metal. Women donated their hair to make bowstrings. Despite heroic efforts, the city was ultimately overwhelmed by the superior Roman army under the command of Scipio Aemilianus (adoptive grandson of Scipio Africanus).

Destruction and Outcome

By 146 BCE, the Romans breached Carthage's walls and fought street by street. The city fell, and according to accounts, Rome razed Carthage to the ground. The survivors were sold into slavery. Legend says the Romans sowed salt into the land to ensure nothing would grow again, although modern historians debate whether that part is literal or symbolic.

With Carthage annihilated, Rome turned the surrounding region into a province named Africa. The destruction of Carthage stands as one of the most brutal acts of total warfare in ancient history. It also signaled Rome's clear dominance over the western Mediterranean—no rival remained.

Consequences and Legacy

1. **Rome's Mediterranean Dominance**: The Punic Wars allowed Rome to become the unrivaled power in the western Mediterranean. Eventually, Rome's attention turned east, and it began to expand into the Hellenistic kingdoms.
2. **Military and Naval Innovations**: Both sides spurred each other to develop new tactics—Rome became adept at naval warfare while also refining land strategies. Carthage continued to innovate with elephants and combined-arms approaches, even if they ultimately lost.
3. **Economic Shifts**: The wars laid waste to large areas of Sicily, Iberia, and North Africa. Rome gained new provinces and sources of wealth, including huge numbers of slaves captured in war. This influx of slaves had profound social and economic impacts on Roman agriculture and society.
4. **Cultural and Psychological Impact**: Rome's victory fueled a sense of pride and superiority. Military success became tied to Rome's identity, accelerating the push for further expansions. Meanwhile, Carthage's destruction served as a cautionary tale of how a once-flourishing city could be erased by conflict.
5. **Hannibal's Legacy**: Even in defeat, Hannibal became a legendary figure, admired for his strategic brilliance. His campaigns in Italy remain some of the most studied military operations in history, illustrating the potential of audacious planning and cunning leadership.

Key Lessons from the Punic Wars

1. **Strategy Over Numbers**: Hannibal showed that cunning strategy could overcome numerical disadvantages, as seen at Cannae.

2. **Logistics and Endurance**: Rome's ability to replace fleets, gather new armies, and secure local alliances outlasted Carthage's resources.
3. **Adaptability**: Both powers changed tactics—Rome from land-based to naval, Carthage employing new leadership and diverse troops—proving the importance of flexibility in warfare.
4. **Total War Consequences**: The final destruction of Carthage demonstrates the extreme end of total war, where the goal is not just victory but the permanent elimination of a rival.

Chapter 6: The Roman Civil Wars and Imperial Expansion

Introduction

By the second century BCE, Rome was the unchallenged master of the western Mediterranean, having triumphed over Carthage in the Punic Wars. However, victory brought new challenges—massive wealth flowed into Rome, generating social inequalities and unrest. Ambitious generals gained popularity and power, at times clashing with the traditional republican system. Over the next two centuries, a series of civil wars and internal conflicts would reshape Rome from a republic governed by elected magistrates and a Senate, into an autocratic empire ruled by emperors.

In this chapter, we will explore how Rome's expansion led to internal strife, focusing on major civil wars and the key figures who fought them. We will see how leaders like Sulla, Julius Caesar, and Augustus used military might, political alliances, and propaganda to advance their agendas. By the end, the Roman world was forever changed, with the republic giving way to the Roman Empire—a transformation that had profound consequences for the ancient world.

The Seeds of Internal Conflict

The Impact of Imperial Growth

Rome's conquest of territories across the Mediterranean brought in vast wealth—land, slaves, and treasure from defeated enemies. Rich aristocratic families acquired huge estates (latifundia), often worked by slaves. Small farmers, unable to compete with large slave-run estates, fell into debt and lost their land. Many drifted to Rome, swelling the city's population of landless citizens.

This social shift created tension between the "haves," represented by the Senatorial elite, and the "have-nots," represented by poorer citizens. Politicians began to capitalize on popular discontent, promising reforms or leveraging fear of social change. Two main political factions emerged in the late republic:

- **Optimates**: The conservative aristocrats who wanted to preserve the traditional privileges of the Senate.
- **Populares**: Leaders who appealed to the masses, often bypassing the Senate and using the people's assemblies to pass laws.

The Gracchi Brothers

Tiberius and Gaius Gracchus, known as the Gracchi, were tribunes in the later second century BCE who tried to address economic inequality by proposing land reforms and other measures to help the poor. Their actions challenged the power of the Senate, leading to violent reactions from conservative elites. Both brothers were killed in political riots. Their deaths marked the beginning of a trend where violence became an accepted tool in Roman politics, foreshadowing more severe conflicts to come.

The Rise of Powerful Generals

Gaius Marius and Military Reforms

Gaius Marius was a populares-aligned general who reformed the Roman army around 107 BCE. Previously, soldiers had to own land and buy their own equipment, which limited recruitment to wealthier citizens. Marius opened the legions to landless citizens, promising pay, loot, and land grants after service. This professionalized the army, but it also created personal loyalty of soldiers to their general rather than to the state. Soldiers now looked to their commander for rewards, setting the stage for generals to wield formidable political power.

Marius gained fame by defeating the Numidian king Jugurtha and later repelling invasions by Germanic tribes such as the Cimbri and Teutones. His popularity soared, and he was elected consul multiple times—an unprecedented break with tradition. However, his career also sparked envy and rivalry among other ambitious politicians.

Lucius Cornelius Sulla

Sulla began as a subordinate of Marius but later emerged as a rival. Skilled, ambitious, and aligned with the optimate faction, he won fame by capturing Jugurtha (under Marius's command) and securing victories in the Social War (91-88 BCE), a conflict between Rome and its Italian allies who sought citizenship rights.

When the Senate gave Sulla the command in a war against King Mithridates of Pontus, a conflict arose because the popular assembly tried to transfer that command to Marius. Sulla marched his legions on Rome—an unprecedented act—seizing the city by force. This was the first time a Roman general had used an army against Rome itself. Sulla then went east, defeated Mithridates, and returned to Rome once again to enforce his agenda.

The First Major Civil War: Sulla vs. Marians (88-82 BCE)

Sulla's March on Rome (88 BCE)

In 88 BCE, when Sulla learned that Marius's supporters stripped him of his command, he refused to submit. Marching his loyal troops into Rome, he occupied the city, driving out his opponents. This violated every norm of the republic, shattering the taboo against using military force within the sacred boundary of Rome (the pomerium). Sulla installed new consuls more favorable to him, then left to fight Mithridates.

Marius' Return and the Marian Faction

With Sulla absent, Marius and his allies reasserted control. Marius died soon after, but the Marian faction continued to hold power, implementing popular reforms and targeting Sulla's supporters. Violence and proscriptions (state-sanctioned killings) became common political tools. Rome experienced waves of terror, with each faction eliminating key rivals when in power.

The Battle for Supremacy

After defeating Mithridates, Sulla returned to Italy in 83 BCE with his seasoned legions. He waged a brutal civil war against the Marian forces. The conflict ended in 82 BCE, when Sulla defeated the last major Marian armies, became dictator, and initiated widespread proscriptions against his enemies. Hundreds of aristocrats and thousands of citizens were killed or exiled, and their properties confiscated.

Sulla's Dictatorship and Reforms

Sulla declared himself dictator legibus faciendis et reipublicae constituendae causa ("dictator to write laws and reorganize the state"). Traditionally, dictators in Rome served short terms in emergencies, but Sulla kept his power for multiple years. He passed reforms to strengthen the Senate and weaken the tribunate, aiming to restore authority to the aristocracy and prevent future popular uprisings.

Surprisingly, Sulla retired voluntarily in 79 BCE and died the following year. Although he stepped down, the precedent of seizing power by force and using proscriptions lingered, foreshadowing future cycles of civil violence.

The Spartacus Revolt (73–71 BCE) and the Rise of Pompey and Crassus

Shortly after Sulla's death, another crisis tested Rome: a massive slave uprising led by Spartacus, a gladiator. Tens of thousands of slaves fled rural estates, forming an army that ravaged parts of Italy. Eventually, Marcus Licinius Crassus, a wealthy aristocrat, took command and defeated the revolt in a brutal campaign. Gnaeus Pompeius Magnus (Pompey the Great) also contributed by mopping up fleeing slave forces, and he took much of the credit in Rome.

Both Crassus and Pompey used this success to gain political leverage. Pompey in particular grew popular due to earlier successes in Spain against Marian remnants. In 70 BCE, both men were elected consuls, despite Pompey being younger than the minimum age. Their joint consulship marked a shift in power—generals with armies wielded huge influence, and the traditional republican checks struggled to contain them.

The Rise of Julius Caesar and the First Triumvirate

Julius Caesar's Background

Julius Caesar, born around 100 BCE, came from the Julian clan, which claimed descent from Venus. Politically aligned with the populares, he was related by marriage to Marius. Caesar carefully navigated the dangerous politics of Sulla's dictatorship by lying low. After Sulla's death, Caesar began a political and military career, quickly gaining a reputation for charisma, oratory skills, and ambition.

The First Triumvirate (60 BCE)

By 60 BCE, Caesar formed a secret alliance with Pompey and Crassus known as the First Triumvirate. Each had something to gain:

- **Pompey**: Wanted land for his veterans and ratification of his settlements in the east.
- **Crassus**: Desired new opportunities to grow wealth and respect, possibly targeting military command in the east.
- **Caesar**: Sought a prestigious command to earn military glory (and pay off debts accrued from lavish public spectacles).

With their combined power, they dominated Roman politics. Caesar secured a consulship in 59 BCE, passed legislation to satisfy Pompey's veterans, and then obtained a long proconsular command in Gaul. For nearly a decade, Caesar waged the Gallic Wars, subjugating much of modern France and parts of Belgium, Germany, and Switzerland, winning enormous wealth and fame.

The Gallic Wars and Growing Tensions

Caesar's Conquests in Gaul

From 58 to 51 BCE, Caesar led Roman legions in a series of campaigns across Gaul. He claimed these were defensive wars—protecting allies or responding to alleged threats. In reality, Caesar aimed to expand Rome's territory, gain personal glory, and secure resources. He famously crossed the Rhine in a show of power, and even made a brief expedition to Britain.

Caesar's success made him popular with the masses in Rome but stirred jealousy among aristocrats. Some senators feared he would use his loyal legions against the state, as Sulla had done. Pompey, once Caesar's ally, grew wary of Caesar's rising star.

The Breakdown of the Triumvirate

The Triumvirate's stability relied on personal bonds and political deals. But when Crassus died in 53 BCE while campaigning against the Parthians, the balance of power shifted. Without Crassus, Caesar and Pompey became outright rivals.

Pompey allied more closely with the Senate and supported moves to limit Caesar's powers, demanding he disband his army before returning to Rome.

The Second Major Civil War: Caesar vs. Pompey (49–45 BCE)

Crossing the Rubicon (49 BCE)

When the Senate ordered Caesar to relinquish command of his legions and return as a private citizen, he faced a dilemma: comply and face possible prosecution by his enemies, or resist and risk civil war. Caesar chose the latter. In 49 BCE, he led his army across the Rubicon River—the boundary of his province—famously declaring "alea iacta est" ("the die is cast"). By crossing this line with troops, Caesar started another civil war.

Early Campaigns

Pompey and many senators fled Italy, heading for Greece to assemble an army. Caesar rapidly took Rome with minimal resistance. He then secured Spain, where many of Pompey's legions were stationed. Caesar's swift action showcased his organizational prowess and the loyalty of his seasoned troops.

The Battle of Pharsalus (48 BCE)

Pompey gathered a large army in the east, supported by the Senate's authority and many Roman nobles. Caesar traveled to Greece, but faced supply issues and was initially outnumbered. Eventually, the two forces clashed at Pharsalus in central Greece in 48 BCE. Despite being at a numerical disadvantage, Caesar's veterans were better trained. Pompey's force was routed; Pompey fled to Egypt, where he was assassinated on orders of Pharaoh Ptolemy XIII, who hoped to please Caesar.

Cleopatra and the Egyptian Campaign

Arriving in Egypt, Caesar was angered by Pompey's murder, seeing it as a dishonorable act. He became embroiled in a dynastic struggle between Ptolemy XIII and his sister Cleopatra VII. Caesar backed Cleopatra, defeating Ptolemy's forces. Cleopatra became Rome's ally (and Caesar's lover), bearing him a son, Caesarion. Caesar spent time consolidating power in the east before returning to Rome.

Mopping Up Opposition

Over the next few years, Caesar crushed remaining opposition in Africa and Spain. By 45 BCE, he was the unchallenged ruler of Rome, assuming the title "Dictator for Life."

Caesar's Assassination and Aftermath

The Ides of March (44 BCE)

Caesar's concentration of power alarmed many senators, including former allies. Fearing Caesar aimed to crown himself king—anathema to Roman republican ideals—a group of senators conspired to kill him. On the Ides of March (March 15, 44 BCE), Caesar was stabbed to death in the Senate. The conspirators, led by Brutus and Cassius, believed they had saved the republic. Instead, they unleashed more chaos.

The Rise of the Second Triumvirate

Following Caesar's murder, Mark Antony (Caesar's loyal lieutenant) and Octavian (Caesar's grandnephew and adopted son) emerged as key players. They, along with Lepidus, formed the Second Triumvirate in 43 BCE. Unlike the first, this triumvirate was legally recognized, and it wielded dictatorial power. They launched proscriptions against their enemies, including Cicero, an influential orator who had aligned with the Senate.

The Third Major Civil War: Antony vs. Octavian (44–31 BCE)

Defeat of the Conspirators

Mark Antony and Octavian marched against the "Liberators," Brutus and Cassius. The conspirators were defeated at the Battles of Philippi in 42 BCE. Brutus and Cassius committed suicide, ending the hopes of a republican restoration. The triumvirs divided the empire among themselves: Lepidus took Africa, Antony ruled the east, and Octavian controlled Italy and the west.

Antony and Cleopatra

Antony made Egypt his base, aligning with Cleopatra. Their relationship became both romantic and political—Antony needed Egypt's wealth to finance campaigns against Parthia and to maintain power in the east. Octavian used Antony's affair with Cleopatra to tarnish his reputation in Rome, claiming Antony had become a slave to an Egyptian queen and was betraying Roman values.

The Final Showdown: The Battle of Actium (31 BCE)

Tensions rose as Antony's enemies in Rome gravitated to Octavian. In 32 BCE, Octavian declared war on Cleopatra (and effectively on Antony). The decisive naval battle occurred at Actium in 31 BCE, off the western coast of Greece. Antony and Cleopatra's combined fleet was outmaneuvered by Octavian's admiral, Agrippa. After a short fight, Cleopatra fled, and Antony followed, leading to the collapse of their forces.

Aftermath: The Dawn of the Roman Empire

Antony and Cleopatra retreated to Egypt and committed suicide in 30 BCE as Octavian's forces closed in. Octavian annexed Egypt, ending the Ptolemaic line. He returned to Rome as the undisputed master of the Mediterranean world. In 27 BCE, he took the title "Augustus," effectively becoming the first Roman Emperor. This marked the end of the republic and the beginning of the Roman Empire.

Imperial Expansion Under Augustus and Beyond

Augustus' Reforms

Augustus maintained the facade of republican institutions—the Senate and traditional offices still existed—but he held the real power. He reorganized the army into a standing force with long-term service, established the Praetorian Guard to secure his authority, and managed the empire's frontiers carefully. Rather than continuous expansion, Augustus aimed for stability, consolidating Roman rule in Spain, Gaul, and the eastern provinces.

Later Emperors

Subsequent emperors continued to expand or defend Roman frontiers:

- **Tiberius and Caligula**: Focused on internal matters but kept the empire mostly stable.
- **Claudius**: Conquered Britain in 43 CE, adding a new province.
- **Trajan** (98–117 CE): Extended Rome to its greatest territorial extent, including Dacia (modern Romania) and parts of the Middle East.

Despite ongoing wars, the biggest threat to Rome after the first century BCE was no longer an external rival like Carthage but rather internal power struggles and, later, pressures on the frontiers from Germanic tribes and Parthians/Sassanids in the east.

Consequences and Legacy of the Civil Wars

1. **End of the Republic**: The republican system, with checks and balances, was effectively dismantled. Power coalesced around a single ruler, setting the stage for centuries of imperial rule.
2. **Professional Army and Personal Loyalties**: Generals like Sulla, Pompey, and Caesar illustrated how troops loyal to a single commander could sway politics. This pattern continued under the emperors, occasionally leading to civil wars when multiple claimants vied for the throne.
3. **Cultural Transformation**: As Rome became an empire, Greek culture mixed more thoroughly into Roman life (especially after interactions with the Hellenistic east). Emperors patronized arts and architecture, leading to monumental buildings that symbolized imperial grandeur.
4. **Administrative Centralization**: Augustus and his successors developed an imperial bureaucracy. Though local traditions were usually tolerated, ultimate control rested in the emperor's hands, supported by a network of loyal officials.
5. **Stability vs. Fragility**: The empire brought relative peace (the Pax Romana), improved infrastructure, and stable governance across vast territories. Yet the system often depended on the emperor's competence. Poor leadership or military disasters could destabilize the entire empire.

Key Lessons from Rome's Internal Wars

1. **Power of Charismatic Generals**: Generals with loyal armies can override political institutions, demonstrating that military loyalty can surpass civic structures.
2. **Importance of Economic and Social Reforms**: Unresolved social inequalities fueled unrest, allowing demagogues and ambitious generals to exploit popular discontent.
3. **Precedent of Violence in Politics**: Once violence became accepted as a political tool (as seen with the Gracchi and Sulla), civil war became more likely.
4. **Adaptability of Political Systems**: Rome's transition from republic to empire was gradual, shaped by the interplay of existing institutions, personal ambition, and societal pressures.
5. **Enduring Impact of Strong Individuals**: Figures like Caesar and Augustus reshaped not just government but also cultural and social norms, leaving a legacy that continued long after their deaths.

Chapter 7: The Wars of the Middle Ages (Part 1) — Byzantium, The Rise of Islam, and the Early Crusades

Introduction

By the end of the Roman Empire in the West (traditionally dated to 476 CE), the eastern half, often called the Byzantine Empire, continued to thrive. Centered in Constantinople (formerly Byzantium), this empire preserved Roman laws and government forms but was also deeply influenced by Greek language and culture. Meanwhile, a dramatic new force emerged in Arabia in the 7th century: Islam, which spread swiftly under the leadership of the Prophet Muhammad's successors, uniting various tribes and forming expansive caliphates. These Islamic powers soon clashed with the Byzantine Empire and the weakened remnants of older Persian powers.

Farther west, Europe was fragmented into smaller kingdoms. Charlemagne's Frankish realm briefly unified parts of western Europe in the 8th and 9th centuries, but after his death, these lands again splintered. Against this backdrop, the Pope's call to reclaim the Holy Land in the late 11th century ignited the Crusades—wars that pulled together knights and peasants under the banner of Christendom. In this chapter, we will focus on Byzantium's early medieval wars, the rapid expansion of Islam, and the First through Third Crusades. We will see how shifting alliances, religious zeal, and political ambitions shaped these conflicts and reshaped the map of the Middle Ages.

Section I: The Byzantine Empire After Rome

Survival and Continuation of the Eastern Empire

When the Western Roman Empire fell, the eastern part survived and evolved into what we now call the Byzantine Empire. The Byzantines considered themselves Romans but spoke primarily Greek and developed a distinct form of Christianity known as Eastern Orthodoxy.

- **Justinian's Ambitions (6th Century)**
  One of the most notable Byzantine emperors was Justinian I (r. 527–565). Determined to restore the old Roman Empire's glory, he launched a series of military campaigns in North Africa, Italy, and parts of southern Spain. His generals, notably Belisarius and Narses, achieved remarkable victories against the Vandals in Africa and the Ostrogoths in Italy. However, these campaigns strained the empire's treasury and manpower.
  Additionally, Justinian is famous for the **Corpus Juris Civilis**, a codification of Roman law, and for constructing the magnificent Hagia Sophia in Constantinople. Despite his conquests, the reconquered western territories proved difficult to hold, partly due to continuous warfare and the outbreak of the Justinianic Plague.
- **Byzantine Defensive Wars**
  After Justinian, the empire often found itself on the defensive. Lombards invaded northern Italy, Slavs pressed into the Balkans, and new threats appeared from the east. Successive emperors struggled to protect diminishing territories, relying on strong walls (like the Theodosian Walls around Constantinople) and mobile field armies. The Byzantines developed a complex system of military districts called "themes," where soldiers received land in exchange for service, supporting local defense.

Section II: The Rise of Islam and Its Early Conquests

Muhammad and the Birth of a New Faith

Islam began in the early 7th century with the preaching of the Prophet Muhammad in Mecca and Medina (in the Arabian Peninsula). After facing opposition in Mecca, Muhammad and his followers migrated to Medina in 622 CE (the Hijra), marking the start of the Islamic calendar. Over the next decade, Muhammad united many Arabian tribes through both diplomacy and warfare. By his death in 632, much of the Arabian Peninsula was under Muslim rule.

- **The Rashidun Caliphate (632–661)**
  Following Muhammad's death, leadership passed to the "Rightly Guided Caliphs" (Abu Bakr, Umar, Uthman, and Ali). Under them, the Muslim community expanded beyond Arabia with extraordinary speed.

- **Conquest of the Levant and Egypt**: Under Caliph Umar, Muslim armies defeated Byzantine forces in Syria at the Battle of Yarmouk (636 CE). This decisive clash opened the Levant (modern-day Syria, Lebanon, Jordan, Israel/Palestine) to Islamic rule. Around the same time, Muslim forces marched into Egypt, capturing key cities like Alexandria.
- **Defeat of the Sasanian Persians**: The final decades of the Sasanian Empire (in modern-day Iran and Iraq) coincided with internal strife. Muslim armies took advantage, defeating the Persians at battles like Qadisiyyah (c. 636 CE) and Nihavand (642 CE), effectively toppling the Sasanian state.

These rapid conquests dramatically shrank the Byzantine Empire, depriving it of prosperous territories in the Near East and North Africa.

The Umayyads and Abbasids

After the Rashidun era, power passed to the Umayyad dynasty (661–750), which moved the capital to Damascus and continued expanding Islamic control across North Africa into the Iberian Peninsula. Later, the Abbasid dynasty (750–1258) shifted the capital to Baghdad, focusing on cultural flourishing while still maintaining large territories—though unity frayed over time. The Umayyad presence in Spain and the Abbasids in Baghdad would define political and cultural developments for centuries, setting the stage for interactions (and conflicts) with Byzantine and European powers.

Section III: Byzantium's Struggles Against Islamic Powers

The First Sieges of Constantinople

The newly formed Islamic caliphates, energized by religious zeal and the promise of wealth, repeatedly pressed into Byzantine lands. Two major attempts to take Constantinople stand out:

1. **Siege of Constantinople (674–678)**
   The Umayyad forces blockaded the city by land and sea. However, Byzantine defenders used the formidable city walls and a secret weapon

called **Greek Fire**—an incendiary substance that burned even on water—to repel enemy ships. The siege failed, and the caliphate withdrew.
2. **Siege of Constantinople (717–718)**
   Under Caliph Sulayman, a massive Muslim force again attacked the empire's capital. Emperor Leo III led the defense, aided by a harsh winter and Bulgarian allies. The attackers faced famine and disease, ultimately retreating in defeat. This failure was a turning point; though Islamic forces continued to hold extensive lands, they could not break Constantinople's defenses.

The Role of Theme Armies and Diplomacy

Over time, the Byzantines adapted. They improved local defense systems (the theme system) and engaged in active diplomacy. They might pay tribute to certain Arab leaders to buy peace or encourage disputes between rival Muslim states to lessen pressure on their borders. The empire's smaller resources forced it to develop cunning strategies, balancing military might with alliances and strategic marriages.

Section IV: The Emergence of the Crusades

Background and Motivations

By the late 11th century, the Byzantine Empire had recovered somewhat, especially under the Macedonian dynasty, and wanted to recapture lost territories. Emperor Alexios I Komnenos, alarmed by the advance of the Seljuk Turks—who had taken much of Anatolia—sent appeals to the West for military aid. At the same time, the Western European feudal states were experiencing religious fervor, combined with the concept of **just war** or a **holy war** to reclaim Jerusalem from Muslim powers.

- **Council of Clermont (1095)**: Pope Urban II delivered a rousing sermon, calling knights and nobles to embark on a holy expedition to help Byzantium and to liberate the Holy Sepulchre in Jerusalem. He promised spiritual rewards, including the remission of sins for those who took up the cross.

The response was overwhelming, leading to the First Crusade. People from various backgrounds—nobles, knights, and commoners—sewed crosses on their clothing and began marching east, motivated by faith, hope of land or plunder, or both.

The People's Crusade

Before the official armies organized, a grassroots movement—led by figures like Peter the Hermit—set out in 1096. Thousands of ill-prepared peasants marched across Europe, causing chaos. Many died en route, especially after clashing with local populations or due to inadequate supplies. Those who reached Asia Minor faced the Seljuk Turks and were easily routed. While tragic, the People's Crusade revealed the widespread eagerness ignited by Urban's call.

Section V: The First Crusade (1096–1099)

Major Leaders and Routes

Official crusader armies organized by nobles and knights departed in separate waves. Notable leaders included Godfrey of Bouillon, Raymond of Toulouse, Bohemond of Taranto, and others. They traveled through routes across Europe, passing Constantinople to be ferried into Asia Minor. Emperor Alexios provided some assistance, but also tried to ensure the returning of lost Byzantine territory, leading to suspicion between the Greeks and the Latin crusaders.

Battles in Asia Minor and the Siege of Antioch

- **Battle of Dorylaion (1097)**
  After helping Byzantium retake Nicaea from the Seljuks, the crusaders marched deeper into Anatolia. At Dorylaion, they faced a large Seljuk force. Despite an ambush, the crusaders held firm and eventually prevailed, opening the route toward Syria.
- **Siege of Antioch (1097–1098)**
  Antioch was a large walled city crucial for controlling northern Syria. The siege took months. Eventually, a traitor within the city helped crusaders scale the walls. Soon after, a relieving Muslim army arrived, turning the crusaders into defenders. Famously, the discovery of the "Holy Lance" (reputed to have pierced Christ's side) boosted crusader morale, leading them to sally forth and defeat the besiegers.

Conquest of Jerusalem (1099)

Finally, the crusaders pressed south to Jerusalem. By then, their ranks were thinned by disease, desertion, and battle losses. The city, controlled by the Fatimid Caliphate of Egypt, fell after a furious siege in July 1099. Crusaders stormed the walls and, as many chroniclers attest, slaughtered a large portion of the inhabitants—Muslim and Jewish alike. Although medieval sources may exaggerate details, there is no doubt it was a bloody conquest.

The success of the First Crusade shocked both Christian and Muslim worlds. Europeans established several states in the Levant, known collectively as the Crusader States or the Latin East: the Kingdom of Jerusalem, County of Edessa, Principality of Antioch, and County of Tripoli.

Section VI: The Second Crusade (1147–1149)

Fall of Edessa and the Call for Help

The County of Edessa was the first crusader state formed and also the first to fall. Surrounded by hostile powers, it had weak defenses and a small Latin population. In 1144, Zengi, a powerful Muslim ruler in Mosul, captured Edessa. The shocking loss sparked a call for a new crusade in the West.

- **Bernard of Clairvaux's Preaching**
  The famous abbot Bernard of Clairvaux championed this new crusade, persuading kings such as Louis VII of France and Conrad III of Germany to take the cross. However, the Second Crusade met with a series of disasters: the German army suffered heavy losses in Anatolia; the French forces fared no better. When they finally reached the Levant, they joined King Baldwin III of Jerusalem in an ill-advised attack on Damascus, which ended in failure.

The Second Crusade did not retake Edessa. The crusaders returned home disgraced. It was a sobering reminder that success was not guaranteed and that Muslim powers had begun to coordinate more effectively against the Latin kingdoms.

Section VII: The Rise of Saladin and The Third Crusade (1189–1192)

Saladin's Unification of Muslim Forces

The late 12th century saw the emergence of one of the most famous Muslim leaders of the era, **Salah ad-Din Yusuf ibn Ayyub**, commonly known as Saladin. Of Kurdish origin, he rose to power in Egypt and Syria, uniting Muslim territories that had previously been divided among competing rulers. Saladin's leadership, diplomacy, and emphasis on jihad to reclaim Jerusalem led to renewed conflict with the Crusader States.

- **Battle of Hattin (1187)**
  The Crusader States, weakened by internal disputes and poor leadership, faced disaster at the Battle of Hattin, near the Sea of Galilee. King Guy of Lusignan led the crusader army into a trap. Saladin's forces cut off water supplies, exhausted the crusaders in the heat, and ultimately crushed them. The True Cross (a revered Christian relic) was captured, and much of the Christian nobility was taken prisoner.

After Hattin, Saladin swiftly recaptured many cities, including Jerusalem itself. Unlike the crusaders in 1099, he largely spared civilian populations.

European Monarchs Respond: The Third Crusade

News of the loss of Jerusalem shocked Europe. Pope Gregory VIII called for a new crusade, led by the most powerful monarchs of the day:

1. **Frederick Barbarossa (Holy Roman Emperor)**: He marched overland but drowned in a river en route, causing most of his forces to scatter.
2. **Richard the Lionheart (King of England)**: A skilled warrior and charismatic leader, he traveled by sea and established himself as the main crusader commander in the Levant.
3. **Philip II (King of France)**: He joined, but conflicts with Richard and poor health led him to return home early.

Richard the Lionheart managed to recapture some key coastal cities, such as Acre. He won a notable victory at the Battle of Arsuf (1191), boosting crusader morale. However, he failed to retake Jerusalem. He and Saladin negotiated a settlement allowing Christian pilgrims access to the holy sites while the city remained under Muslim control. Richard returned to Europe in 1192, ending the Third Crusade. Though often romanticized, it achieved limited results compared to the First Crusade.

Section VIII: Consequences and Legacy of the Early Crusades

1. **Cultural Exchanges**: Even though the crusaders and local Muslim forces fought bitterly, these wars opened channels for trade and the exchange of knowledge. Europeans encountered advanced sciences, medicine, and philosophy in the Islamic world, contributing to Europe's intellectual revival in later centuries.
2. **Byzantine Distrust**: Relations between Byzantium and the Latin West worsened. The crusaders often acted with suspicion and arrogance in Byzantine lands, and the Byzantines sometimes withheld full support. This mutual distrust would have severe consequences in future crusades.
3. **Military Orders**: The Templars, Hospitallers, and Teutonic Knights emerged as military orders combining monastic and knightly roles. They protected pilgrims and fought in the Holy Land, eventually becoming powerful organizations with property across Europe.
4. **Changing Power in the Levant**: The Crusader States survived but were increasingly vulnerable, relying on constant reinforcement from Europe. Muslim unity under capable leaders like Saladin proved a formidable challenge.
5. **Religious Motivations vs. Political Gains**: The crusades showcased a blend of religious devotion and personal ambition. Some participants were driven by genuine faith, others by the lure of land, wealth, or power.

Chapter 8: The Wars of the Middle Ages (Part 2) — Late Crusades, Mongol Invasions, and European Feudal Conflicts

Introduction

The First three Crusades dealt huge blows to both European and Middle Eastern powers and deeply affected the Byzantine Empire. Yet the crusading movement did not end with Richard the Lionheart's departure. Subsequent crusades grew more entangled in European politics and often targeted rival Christian cities as well as Muslim states. Meanwhile, from the vast steppes of Mongolia, a new threat emerged: the Mongols, led initially by Genghis Khan, carved out the largest contiguous land empire in history. Their swift invasions took both Asian and European powers by surprise. Back in Western Europe, feudal kingdoms and principalities engaged in constant local struggles, driven by shifting alliances and dynastic ambitions.

In this chapter, we will examine the Fourth through later Crusades, focusing on how they deviated from initial goals and caused lasting tensions between Latin Christians and Byzantines. We will then analyze the Mongol conquests—from China to Eastern Europe—and the drastic impact these invasions had on older states. Finally, we will look at key European feudal conflicts leading into the late medieval period, setting the stage for momentous wars like the Hundred Years' War in the following chapter. Together, these conflicts shaped medieval society and politics, leaving behind a complex legacy of cultural exchange, devastation, and transformation.

Section I: The Fourth Crusade (1202–1204) and Its Aftermath

Diverted to Constantinople

Pope Innocent III called for a new crusade to strike at Egypt, then the main seat of Muslim power under the Ayyubid Dynasty (descendants of Saladin's empire). However, financial problems led the crusaders to make a deal with the Republic of Venice: the Venetians would transport the crusader army by sea in exchange for payment. When the crusaders struggled to raise the required funds, Venice demanded alternative compensation—such as helping subdue Zara (a Christian city and commercial rival on the Adriatic).

Meanwhile, a Byzantine prince, Alexios Angelos, promised the crusaders riches and religious union with Rome if they helped him reclaim the throne in Constantinople. Seduced by the possibility of wealth, the crusaders accepted. After a series of political intrigues, the crusaders attacked Constantinople itself in 1203–1204. They sacked the city in April 1204, unleashing destruction on an unprecedented scale. Libraries, churches, and palaces were looted. Precious relics were carried off to Western Europe, and many of Constantinople's citizens faced violence and pillage.

- **Impact of the Sack**: The crusaders established a **Latin Empire** in Constantinople, while other powers carved out territories in Greece. This severely weakened Byzantium, which survived in exile states like Nicaea and Epirus. Relations between the Orthodox East and Catholic West deteriorated further. The Orthodox inhabitants felt deeply betrayed, and the schism between the two branches of Christianity widened.

Diminished Aims and Legacy

With Constantinople under Latin control, the original goal of attacking Egypt was essentially forgotten. Pope Innocent III was dismayed by the turn of events but eventually accepted the new Latin Empire. Over time, Byzantine exiles in Nicaea and elsewhere regrouped, and by 1261, the Greeks recaptured Constantinople under Emperor Michael VIII Palaiologos. Nevertheless, the once-mighty empire never fully recovered from the Fourth Crusade's devastation.

Section II: Other Later Crusades

The Fifth Crusade (1217–1221)

Determined to refocus on Egypt as the key to controlling the Holy Land, Pope Honorius III launched the Fifth Crusade. Led initially by King Andrew II of Hungary and Duke Leopold VI of Austria, the crusaders captured the port of Damietta in Egypt in 1219. However, their attempt to advance further to Cairo was thwarted by rising Nile floodwaters, logistic failures, and strong resistance from the Ayyubids. They had to surrender Damietta and withdraw.

The Sixth Crusade (1228–1229)

Remarkably, this crusade was led by Emperor Frederick II of the Holy Roman Empire, who had clashed with the papacy. Frederick negotiated with Sultan al-Kamil of Egypt, securing a peaceful handover of Jerusalem, Nazareth, and Bethlehem to Christian control. This diplomatic outcome angered some crusaders who wanted a glorious military campaign. Nevertheless, Frederick crowned himself King of Jerusalem and left soon after, illustrating how the crusading ideal had splintered into personal ambition and realpolitik.

The Seventh and Eighth Crusades (1248–1254; 1270)

French King Louis IX (later canonized as Saint Louis) led both of these expeditions, focusing again on Egypt. The Seventh Crusade captured Damietta but ended in Louis's defeat and capture. A significant ransom was paid, and the crusaders withdrew. The Eighth Crusade targeted Tunisia but ended with Louis's death from illness. Neither significantly advanced the crusader cause.

Decline of Crusader States

By the late 13th century, crusader strongholds in the Levant fell one by one to Mamluk forces (the Mamluks had replaced the Ayyubids in Egypt). Acre, the last major crusader city, was captured in 1291, effectively ending the Frankish presence in the Holy Land. Although minor attempts to retake territory continued sporadically, the era of large-scale crusades to the Levant had come to a close.

Section III: The Mongol Invasions (13th–14th Centuries)

The Rise of Genghis Khan

While the Europeans and Middle Eastern states struggled with crusades and regional power shifts, a storm brewed on the eastern steppes. Temüjin, better known as Genghis Khan, united the Mongol tribes around 1206 and launched campaigns that would shock the world. The Mongol armies, famed for their swift horse archers and brutal tactics, conquered vast territories with unprecedented speed.

- **Conquest of Central Asia and Persia**: Genghis Khan subdued the Khwarezmian Empire in Persia after a diplomatic incident enraged him. Mongol forces razed cities like Bukhara and Samarkand. Survivors were often enslaved or forced into Mongol armies as labor troops.
- **Northern China**: Genghis Khan also turned on the Jin Dynasty in northern China. The Mongols perfected siege warfare by capturing Chinese engineers, learning to use catapults and gunpowder bombs.

By Genghis Khan's death in 1227, the Mongol Empire spanned from the Pacific coast of Asia to Eastern Europe's doorstep.

The Invasion of Europe

Genghis Khan's successors continued expansion. Under Ogedei Khan, Mongol armies surged westward:

1. **Battle of Kalka River (1223)**
   An exploratory Mongol force defeated a combined Russian and Kipchak army in the steppes north of the Black Sea. This victory signaled the Mongols' potential threat to eastern Europe.
2. **The Great Western Campaign (1236–1242)**
   Led by Batu Khan and Subutai, the Mongols conquered the Volga Bulgars, devastated the principalities of Rus', and annihilated Polish and Hungarian armies at battles like Legnica (1241) and Mohi (1241). Europeans were terrified by the Mongols' unstoppable advance and brutal devastation. Only the death of the Great Khan Ogedei forced Batu Khan to withdraw to select a new Mongol leader, sparing western Europe from likely invasion at that time.

The Mongols in the Middle East

Another Mongol branch, led by Hulagu Khan, grandson of Genghis Khan, advanced into the Middle East:

- **Destruction of the Abbasid Caliphate (1258)**: Hulagu captured Baghdad, a center of Islamic civilization. The city was sacked, and the last Abbasid caliph was executed. The Tigris supposedly ran black from the ink of countless destroyed manuscripts, and red from the blood of the slain.
- **Battle of Ain Jalut (1260)**: Mongol forces advanced into Syria, but the Mamluks of Egypt decisively defeated a Mongol army at Ain Jalut. This

battle is famously regarded as the first major Mongol defeat in open combat and is credited with stopping the Mongol advance into North Africa.

Mongol Legacy and Fragmentation

The vast Mongol Empire eventually split into khanates, such as the Golden Horde in Russia, the Ilkhanate in Persia, the Chagatai Khanate in Central Asia, and the Yuan Dynasty in China (founded by Kublai Khan, Genghis's grandson). Over time, these entities adapted to local cultures, converted to Islam or Buddhism, and lost the unity that once made the Mongols so formidable. The Mongol period, however, greatly affected trade across Eurasia (encouraging East-West exchange via the Silk Road) but also devastated countless cities, changing demographic and political landscapes for centuries.

Section IV: Feudal Conflicts in Medieval Europe

Feudalism and Warfare

In medieval Europe, power was decentralized. Kings, dukes, counts, and knights held lands in a system of mutual obligations known as feudalism. Lords granted fiefs (land) to vassals in return for military service. War was frequent and often local, involving sieges of castles or pitched battles between feudal hosts. Knights, clad in heavy armor and mounted on warhorses, dominated the battlefield, although infantry and archers also played important roles.

Conflicts in the Holy Roman Empire and Italy

The Holy Roman Empire encompassed present-day Germany, Austria, parts of Italy, and other regions. Emperors, such as Frederick Barbarossa, struggled to assert control over the Italian city-states, which fiercely guarded their independence. Northern Italian communes (like Milan, Florence, Venice) often formed leagues (e.g., the Lombard League) to resist imperial influence. These ongoing wars and rebellions shaped the political map of Italy, with cities forming alliances against emperors or each other.

Anglo-French Rivalries Before the Hundred Years' War

Tensions between England and France simmered even before the famous Hundred Years' War (which began in 1337). English kings held substantial lands in

France (the Angevin Empire of the Plantagenet kings, for instance). Disputes over feudal allegiance, control of territories such as Normandy and Aquitaine, and claims to the French throne led to a series of smaller conflicts and shifting alliances.

- **Battle of Bouvines (1214)**: A pivotal medieval battle in which French King Philip II (Augustus) defeated an alliance of English, Flemish, and German forces. This cemented Capetian control over much of northern France and pushed back English dominion on the continent.

The Reconquista in the Iberian Peninsula

As the Umayyads established al-Andalus in southern Spain in the early 8th century, Christian kingdoms in the north (Asturias, Leon, Castile, Aragon) gradually pushed south over centuries, a process known as the Reconquista. This long struggle involved both warfare and cultural interaction. Occasionally, Christian and Muslim princes allied against common foes. Major turning points included the Battle of Las Navas de Tolosa (1212), where Christian forces dealt a severe blow to the Almohad caliphate. By the late 13th century, only the Emirate of Granada remained in Muslim hands, until it fell in 1492—beyond the main scope of our current discussion.

Section V: Military and Technological Innovations of the High Middle Ages

1. **Castles and Fortifications**: Nobles invested heavily in stone castles, serving both as residences and defensive strongpoints. Sieges became a central part of medieval warfare; attackers developed battering rams, siege towers, trebuchets, and mining techniques to breach walls.
2. **Knighthood and Chivalry**: Mounted knights were symbols of power and prestige. Tournaments, jousts, and the code of chivalry shaped aristocratic culture. However, the reality of war was often far from chivalrous, with brutal raids and pillaging.
3. **Crossbows and Longbows**: Advances in archery changed battlefield dynamics. The crossbow, though slower to reload, had strong penetrating power. The longbow (especially famous in English hands) had a faster rate of fire and could outshoot many conventional bows.

4. **Gunpowder's Early Introduction**: By the 14th century, gunpowder weapons, like small cannons and primitive handgunnery, began appearing in Europe—an innovation transmitted from East Asia through Islamic lands. Although not yet decisive in early use, gunpowder would eventually revolutionize warfare in the late Middle Ages.

Section VI: Impacts and Shifts Toward the Late Middle Ages

1. **Fragmentation vs. Centralization**: While feudal lords clashed over local issues, certain monarchies (like France and England) gradually strengthened royal institutions. This set the stage for future nation-states.
2. **Trade and Economic Growth**: Despite wars, trade routes flourished in some regions, especially in the Italian maritime republics (Venice, Genoa) and the Hanseatic League in northern Europe. Wealth from commerce funded armies and influenced political power.
3. **Cultural Interactions**: Both the crusading movement and the Mongol Empire facilitated exchanges of knowledge, goods, and ideas. European courts acquired Greek and Arabic texts via translations, enriching philosophy, science, and medicine.
4. **Shift of Warfare Norms**: Interactions with Muslim armies in the Levant and North Africa, as well as with steppe nomads, taught Europeans new tactics and technologies. At the same time, religious motivations for war sometimes gave way to more secular aims of territory and power.

Section VII: Key Lessons from the Later Crusades and Mongol Invasions

1. **Unintended Outcomes**: The Fourth Crusade's sack of Constantinople demonstrated how crusaders could be diverted from official objectives, leading to actions that undercut broader Christian unity.
2. **Diplomatic and Strategic Complexities**: Kingdoms and states frequently allied with former enemies or employed mercenaries from distant lands when convenient. Pragmatism often overrode piety or ideology.

3. **Mobility and Adaptation**: The Mongols showcased the supreme value of mobility, discipline, and advanced siege techniques. Opponents who failed to adapt often succumbed quickly.
4. **Cultural and Economic Exchange**: Despite conflict, these wars opened pathways for trade and intellectual growth, bridging East and West in both violent and peaceful ways.

Chapter 9: The Hundred Years' War

Introduction

The Hundred Years' War (1337-1453) was a long, complicated struggle between England and France over claims to the French throne, territorial disputes, and feudal loyalties. Although we refer to it as a single war, it consisted of several periods of fighting interrupted by truces and uneasy peace treaties. This conflict brought forth legendary battles, significant changes in warfare, and figures like Joan of Arc who reshaped the course of European history.

In this chapter, we will examine the roots of the conflict, key phases of the war, major battles, diplomatic efforts, and the eventual outcome that redefined both the French and English monarchies. We will also look at how the war impacted ordinary people, introduced new military tactics, and gradually changed ideas about kingship and national identity.

Section I: Background and Causes

Feudal Loyalties and Dynastic Claims

To understand why the Hundred Years' War started, we must look at the feudal system linking England and France in the early 14th century. Since the Norman Conquest (1066), English kings held lands in France. Over time, these territories—Aquitaine, Gascony, and others—varied in size and importance but remained under the English monarch's control as vassals of the French king. This arrangement caused constant friction, as the French crown often tried to curb English power on the continent, and the English resented paying homage to another monarch.

A second major cause was **dynastic**. The French royal line, the Capetians, faced a succession crisis when Charles IV of France died in 1328 without a surviving son. According to strict feudal custom, property or titles could pass through a female line under certain circumstances, but French nobles invoked the so-called **Salic Law**—a tradition stating that the French crown could not descend through a woman. This excluded Edward III of England, whose mother was Isabella, a

French princess and sister of Charles IV. However, Edward III believed he had a legitimate claim to the French throne, sparking intense political tensions. The French nobility instead crowned Philip VI (a cousin of the late king). Edward III eventually pressed his own claim, fueling a confrontation that spiraled into a prolonged war.

Tensions Over Flanders and Trade

Flanders (in modern Belgium) was a vital economic region known for its cloth-making industry, dependent on English wool. The Count of Flanders was a French vassal, but many Flemish towns favored an alliance with England to keep the flow of wool steady. When Philip VI tried to assert direct control over Flanders, local burghers resisted, seeking help from England. This commercial and political discord added more kindling to an already volatile situation.

Section II: The Early Phases (1337–1360)

The Edwardian War

Historians often call the first stage of the conflict the **Edwardian War** (1337–1360), referencing King Edward III of England. Edward's decision to press his claim to the French throne and his alliances with rebellious Flemish cities set the war's initial tone.

1. **Naval Superiority and the Battle of Sluys (1340)**
   Early on, Edward recognized the importance of controlling the English Channel to prevent a French invasion of England and to allow English forces to land in France at will. At the naval battle of Sluys in 1340, off the Flemish coast, the English fleet scored a major victory against the French. Though ship-to-ship combat in the Middle Ages was often chaotic, English longbowmen on decks proved devastating. This victory gave England command of the seas, making it easier for Edward to transport armies across the Channel.
2. **Campaigns in Brittany and Gascony**
   English forces also fought in Brittany, a semi-independent duchy on France's northwest coast, and in Gascony, in southwestern France. In these regions, local lords had their own reasons for supporting or resisting English claims. Skirmishes, sieges, and localized battles were common, with neither side gaining a definitive advantage initially.

3. **The Battle of Crécy (1346)**
   One of the most famous medieval battles, Crécy saw Edward III lead a smaller English army against a larger French force under Philip VI. The English relied heavily on longbowmen. Positioned on a slope, the English archers unleashed volley after volley. French knights, weighed down by armor, advanced in disorganized waves and were decimated by arrows. Rain-soaked crossbows used by French mercenaries failed to match the English rate of fire. The decisive English victory stunned Europe, showing that disciplined longbow units and defensive positioning could overcome a numerically superior cavalry charge.
4. **Siege of Calais (1346–1347)**
   Immediately after Crécy, Edward marched north and laid siege to Calais, a strategic port on the Channel. The siege lasted nearly a year. Calais finally surrendered to the English in 1347. This port became a crucial English outpost on French soil for over two centuries, giving England a stable foothold for further campaigns and a prime location for trade and resupply.

The Black Death and Temporary Lulls

In 1348, the **Black Death** ravaged Europe, drastically reducing populations in both England and France. Armies lost soldiers to the plague, and entire villages were wiped out. This catastrophe caused a temporary slowdown in warfare as leaders and common folk struggled with the pandemic's devastating impact. Although fighting did not cease completely, the scale of campaigns was reduced for a time.

The Battle of Poitiers (1356) and the Capture of a French King

When major campaigns resumed, Edward's son, the **Black Prince** (Edward, Prince of Wales), led significant expeditions into southern and central France. In 1356, at the **Battle of Poitiers**, he faced King John II of France. Again, English longbowmen and dismounted knights formed a defensive line. French cavalry attacks floundered, and King John II himself was captured. The humiliation of losing a king to the enemy caused turmoil in France, leading to heavy ransom demands from the English.

The Treaty of Brétigny (1360)

The capture of King John II forced the French to negotiate. The **Treaty of Brétigny** (1360) favored England. France agreed to cede large territories in southwestern France (expanding English Gascony) and pay a massive ransom for King John's release. In return, Edward III temporarily dropped his claim to the French throne. This treaty ended the first phase of the war, but the peace would not last.

Section III: The Caroline War (1369–1389)

French Revival Under Charles V

King John II died in captivity, and his son **Charles V** (also known as Charles the Wise) inherited a troubled kingdom. Despite earlier defeats, Charles V proved a cautious and effective leader. He appointed the cunning general **Bertrand du Guesclin** to rebuild the French military. Instead of meeting the English in open battle—where longbowmen excelled—Charles and du Guesclin favored skirmishes, raids, and the recapture of key towns through sieges or diplomacy.

- **Avoiding Major Battles**: The French learned from their disastrous defeats at Crécy and Poitiers, adopting more flexible tactics. They used small, mobile forces to harass English garrisons, disrupt supply lines, and retake castles one by one.
- **Economic Pressures**: Maintaining large armies in France was expensive for the English. As local populations turned hostile, English garrisons had to purchase supplies at high prices or resort to pillaging, which further alienated the French.
- **Gradual Loss of English Holdings**: By the late 1370s, France had recaptured much of the territory granted to England under the Treaty of Brétigny, except for Calais and some southwestern coastal areas.

Internal Struggles and Truces

Though the French made gains, they also faced internal challenges. Local revolts, noble rivalries, and the cost of constant warfare were serious burdens. England, for its part, struggled with the high cost of campaigns in France, political tensions at home, and eventual leadership changes. When Edward III died in 1377, his ten-year-old grandson, Richard II, became king. Richard's regents and advisors had varying views on war policy, leading to political infighting.

A series of truces punctuated the Caroline War. Neither side could sustain non-stop conflict, and both used breaks to reorganize. By the late 1380s, the war's second phase ended in relative stalemate. Charles V's death left France in the hands of his son, Charles VI, who would become infamous for his bouts of mental illness. England under Richard II also turned inward, dealing with political strife that would eventually lead to Richard's downfall.

Section IV: The Lancastrian War (1415–1453)

Henry V's Ambitions

The final and most dramatic stage of the Hundred Years' War is often referred to as the **Lancastrian War**, named after the ruling house of Lancaster in England. In 1399, Henry IV deposed Richard II, establishing the Lancastrian branch on the throne. His son, **Henry V** (r. 1413–1422), inherited a kingdom recently stabilized from internal strife. Henry V was determined to reassert English claims in France, perhaps inspired by the glories of Edward III and the Black Prince.

1. **Reopening the War**: In 1415, Henry V launched an invasion, claiming that the French crown had not honored earlier treaties. He landed in Normandy with a well-prepared army. His timing was good: France was plagued by internal divisions, particularly between the royal family (supporters of Charles VI) and the powerful dukes of Burgundy and Orléans.
2. **Battle of Agincourt (1415)**: On October 25, Henry's forces, weakened by disease and short on supplies, found themselves near Agincourt confronted by a much larger French army. Relying once again on longbowmen and a strong defensive position, the English routed the French knights. Casualties among the French nobility were devastating. Agincourt became a legend in English lore, cementing Henry V's reputation as a brilliant commander.

The Treaty of Troyes (1420)

Following more campaigning, the French court, racked by civil war between Burgundian and Armagnac (Orléans) factions, agreed to negotiate with Henry V. Under the **Treaty of Troyes (1420)**:

- Henry V married Catherine of Valois, daughter of Charles VI.
- Henry was recognized as regent and heir to the French throne, disinheriting the Dauphin (the future Charles VII).
- The English gained control of northern France, including Paris.

This astonishing agreement seemed to place the crowns of both England and France on Henry's head upon Charles VI's death, theoretically uniting the two kingdoms.

The Deaths of Henry V and Charles VI

Henry V continued campaigns but died suddenly in 1422 of illness. Just weeks later, Charles VI also died. Under the Treaty of Troyes, Henry V's infant son, Henry VI, was proclaimed King of France and England, with regents ruling in his place. Meanwhile, the disinherited Dauphin (Charles VII) remained in the south, still claiming the French crown. The stage was set for the final struggle over legitimate kingship in France.

Section V: Joan of Arc and the Turning Tide

The Siege of Orléans (1428–1429)

English and Burgundian forces pushed into the Loire Valley, besieging Orléans, a strategic city loyal to Charles VII. If Orléans fell, central and southern France would be wide open. The city's defenders fought bravely but faced grim prospects. Meanwhile, the young peasant woman **Joan of Arc** arrived at Charles VII's court, claiming divine visions that instructed her to drive out the English and see Charles crowned at Reims.

Joan convinced Charles and his advisors to let her join the relief army. Her presence and unwavering faith inspired French troops. In a series of attacks in the spring of 1429, the French broke the siege, forcing the English to retreat. This stunning victory at Orléans raised French morale and turned Joan of Arc into a folk hero almost overnight.

The Coronation at Reims (1429)

Buoyed by momentum, Joan urged Charles to proceed to Reims, the traditional coronation site for French kings. Many towns along the route, seeing the tide shifting, opened their gates to Charles. In July 1429, Charles was crowned Charles VII at Reims Cathedral, with Joan of Arc by his side. This ceremony gave Charles VII the symbolic legitimacy he had lacked under the terms of the Treaty of Troyes.

Joan's Capture and Execution (1430–1431)

Despite early successes, the war was far from over. In May 1430, while defending Compiègne, Joan was captured by Burgundian forces. The Burgundians sold her to the English, who put her on trial for heresy and witchcraft. She was convicted and burned at the stake in 1431 in Rouen. Joan's death was a tragedy for the French cause, but her martyrdom further galvanized French resistance, and the impression she left on both French soldiers and the broader population endured.

Section VI: The Final Victory of France

The Decline of English Power in France

Even without Joan, the French slowly gained ground. Charles VII reorganized his army, improved tax collection to fund professional forces, and formed better artillery units. Meanwhile, England faced financial strain and political instability. Henry VI was a child and would later struggle with mental health issues, leading to factional fighting at home (which would help spark the Wars of the Roses).

- **Reconciliation with Burgundy**: The Duke of Burgundy, a key English ally, gradually shifted allegiance to Charles VII. The **Treaty of Arras (1435)** brought Burgundy back into the French fold, isolating the English.
- **Artillery Revolution**: The French embraced new siege guns and cannons, using them effectively against English-held castles. Over time, they dismantled English strongholds that had once been nearly impossible to breach.

Key French Offensives

In the 1440s and 1450s, Charles VII pushed methodically to reconquer Normandy and Gascony. Major successes included:

- **Battle of Formigny (1450)**: French artillery contributed to a decisive victory over English forces in Normandy.
- **Battle of Castillon (1453)**: Often marked as the final conflict of the Hundred Years' War, Castillon saw French cannons wreak havoc on an English army attempting to relieve a siege. The English commander, John Talbot, was killed, and the remaining English-held territory collapsed. By the end of 1453, all that remained in English hands was the port of Calais.

Section VII: Consequences and Significance

1. **National Consciousness**: Though medieval people typically identified more with local lords than with a broader nation, the Hundred Years' War helped foster an early sense of French unity. In England, the conflict contributed to a growing awareness of "Englishness" as well, though full national identities would emerge gradually over centuries.
2. **Military Evolution**: The longbow played a significant role in English victories, challenging the dominance of heavily armored knights. Meanwhile, the French adoption of large-scale artillery revolutionized siege warfare. Over time, professional armies started to replace feudal levies, laying groundwork for standing armies in the early modern era.
3. **Political Centralization**: In both countries, royal governments grew stronger. In France, the monarchy asserted more direct authority after expelling the English, collecting taxes more efficiently. In England, the monarchy discovered new ways to raise funds (often through Parliament), which both strengthened and strained royal-Parliament relations.
4. **Economic and Social Costs**: The war devastated many regions, especially in France where marauding armies repeatedly ravaged the countryside. Trade suffered, and peasants in contested areas endured repeated hardships. Population displacement occurred, and the cost of warfare fueled higher taxes, sometimes leading to revolts.

5. **End of the Middle Ages for England and France?**: Some historians see 1453, the war's end, as part of the transition to early modern Europe. France emerged more unified under the Valois kings, while England soon fell into internal conflict: the **Wars of the Roses**.

Chapter 10: The Wars of the Roses

Introduction

England emerged from the Hundred Years' War in 1453 having lost almost all its French possessions. Shortly thereafter, the kingdom plunged into a series of internal battles known as the **Wars of the Roses** (1455–1487). This prolonged civil strife involved two rival branches of the royal House of Plantagenet: the House of Lancaster, symbolized by a red rose, and the House of York, symbolized by a white rose. The conflict arose from disputes over succession, the weak leadership of King Henry VI, and powerful nobles vying for influence.

In this chapter, we will trace the origins of the Wars of the Roses, highlight the major battles and power shifts, and see how figures like Richard Neville ("the Kingmaker"), Edward IV, and Richard III shaped the course of English history. We will also examine how the wars ended with the rise of the Tudor dynasty, which brought a semblance of stability after decades of turmoil.

Section I: Background and Political Tensions

Weak Kingship of Henry VI

Henry VI (r. 1422–1461, 1470–1471) inherited the throne as an infant. He was recognized as King of both England and France under the Treaty of Troyes, but as we saw, France was effectively lost by 1453. Henry, deeply religious and mild-mannered, lacked the forceful character needed to manage powerful nobles. Worse still, he experienced bouts of mental incapacity, leaving a vacuum of leadership that ambitious lords rushed to fill.

Powerful Nobles and Factionalism

In late medieval England, the royal court and council were filled with influential men who commanded private armies and held vast estates. Two key figures emerged:

1. **Richard, Duke of York**: A prominent Plantagenet with his own claim to the throne through the Mortimer line. He served as Protector of the Realm during Henry VI's periods of incapacity. Richard believed he had a stronger right to the crown than Henry's Lancastrian line.
2. **Edmund Beaufort, Duke of Somerset**: A leading Lancastrian courtier closely tied to Henry VI and the royal family. He and Richard of York clashed repeatedly over policy and influence at court.

Personal rivalries, disputes over royal favor, and a failing economy fueled tensions. Meanwhile, Henry VI's wife, **Margaret of Anjou**, acted as a fierce defender of the Lancastrian cause, determined to safeguard her husband's crown for their son, Prince Edward.

Section II: The Outbreak of War (1455–1460)

First Battle of St Albans (1455)

Hostilities erupted openly in May 1455 at **St Albans**, a town north of London. The Duke of York's forces defeated a royal army led by the Duke of Somerset, who was killed in the fighting. King Henry VI was wounded and captured, effectively handing control of the government to Richard of York once more. This skirmish is usually cited as the first armed clash of the Wars of the Roses.

Shifting Power and Political Maneuvers

Over the next few years, the balance of power shifted as Henry VI briefly recovered from his mental troubles. Margaret of Anjou worked tirelessly to undermine Richard of York's influence. However, when Henry relapsed, York again served as Protector. The realm seemed caught in a cycle of councils, regencies, and royal charters that seldom lasted more than a few months.

Battle of Blore Heath and Ludford Bridge (1459)

In 1459, fighting resumed. At **Blore Heath**, the Yorkists under Richard Neville, Earl of Salisbury, won a minor victory against Lancastrian forces. But later that year at **Ludford Bridge**, near Ludlow, York's army disintegrated when many troops deserted, unwilling to fight the king directly. Richard of York fled to

Ireland, while his eldest son Edward (the future Edward IV) and other Yorkist lords escaped to Calais.

During this period, the Lancastrian court in Coventry accused the Yorkists of treason, stripping them of titles and lands. In response, the Yorkist leaders consolidated their positions abroad, gathering resources for a return to England.

Section III: Yorkist Ascendancy (1460–1461)

The Invasion of 1460

In June 1460, Richard Neville, Earl of Warwick—nicknamed "the Kingmaker" for his ability to make and unmake kings—led a Yorkist force from Calais back into England. They entered London with minimal resistance, as many residents disliked the heavy-handed Lancastrian regime. Soon, the Yorkists met the royal army at **Northampton** (July 1460). King Henry VI was captured again, and Margaret of Anjou fled north with the prince.

Act of Accord and Richard of York's Claim

With Henry VI under Yorkist control, Parliament passed the **Act of Accord** (October 1460). This declared Henry VI would remain king for his lifetime but recognized Richard of York and his heirs as next in line, effectively disinheriting Prince Edward of Lancaster. Margaret of Anjou rejected this compromise, seeing it as an illegal usurpation of her son's birthright.

The Battle of Wakefield (December 1460)

The Lancastrians regrouped in the north. Richard of York marched to meet them but was unexpectedly overwhelmed at **Wakefield** in December 1460. Richard himself died in the fighting, along with his second son, Edmund, Earl of Rutland. The Duke of York's severed head was displayed on the city gates of York, mocking his earlier ambitions.

This catastrophe did not end the Yorkist cause, however. Richard's eldest son, Edward, now inherited his father's claims.

Section IV: Edward IV and the Triumph of the House of York

Battles of Mortimer's Cross and the Second Battle of St Albans (1461)

Early 1461 saw two critical clashes:

1. **Mortimer's Cross (February 1461)**: Edward, now Duke of York, defeated a Lancastrian force in the Welsh Marches. A rare meteorological event occurred that morning, with three suns appearing in the sky (a phenomenon called a "sun dog"). Edward took it as a sign of divine favor, adopting the symbol of the "Sun in Splendour" thereafter.
2. **Second Battle of St Albans (February 1461)**: Margaret of Anjou led a strong Lancastrian army south, surprising and defeating the Earl of Warwick. Crucially, Margaret recovered King Henry VI, who had been Warwick's captive. However, the Lancastrians failed to capitalize on this victory by not marching on London, possibly due to fear of the city's hostility.

Edward IV's Coronation and the Battle of Towton (March 1461)

Seizing the moment, Edward of York entered London and had himself proclaimed **King Edward IV**. Only 18 years old, he quickly gathered forces to confront the main Lancastrian army in Yorkshire. On **Palm Sunday, March 29, 1461**, the opposing sides met at the **Battle of Towton**, often considered the largest and bloodiest engagement of the Wars of the Roses. Estimates of those involved vary widely, but tens of thousands clashed in a fierce snowstorm.

- **Yorkist Victory**: Edward's forces, aided by strategic use of archers and favorable wind, routed the Lancastrians. Many Lancastrians were killed as they fled across the River Cock, drowning or cut down by pursuers.
- **Aftermath**: Towton secured Edward IV's hold on the throne, at least in southern and central England. Henry VI and Margaret of Anjou escaped to Scotland, continuing to resist from the fringes.

Section V: Edward IV's Reign and the Rise of the "Kingmaker"

Lancastrian Resistance and Margaret's Campaigns

Although Edward IV held London and was crowned in June 1461, significant parts of northern England and Wales remained under Lancastrian influence. Margaret made attempts to rally support in Scotland and France, hoping for foreign aid to restore Henry VI. These efforts led to sporadic rebellions, but none posed a major threat to Edward's rule in the early 1460s.

Richard Neville's Influence

Richard Neville, Earl of Warwick—the "Kingmaker"—had been instrumental in placing Edward on the throne. As Edward's chief supporter, Warwick expected influence over royal policy, including foreign alliances and noble appointments. However, Edward IV began to assert his independence:

- **Marriage to Elizabeth Woodville**: In 1464, Edward secretly married Elizabeth Woodville, a commoner and widow of a Lancastrian knight. This alliance shocked the court, especially Warwick, who had been negotiating a French match for Edward. The Woodville family rapidly gained favors and titles, angering older nobles.

Growing Rift Between Edward IV and Warwick

By 1467, Warwick's dissatisfaction with Edward IV's rule intensified. He disapproved of Edward's preference for an alliance with Burgundy over France. Further fueling tensions, Edward promoted Elizabeth Woodville's relatives, sidelining Warwick's family. This conflict became personal and political, driving Warwick to reconsider his loyalty to the Yorkist king he had helped create.

Section VI: Warwick's Rebellion and the Return of Henry VI

Alliance with Margaret of Anjou

In a remarkable turnaround, Warwick allied with his old enemy, **Margaret of Anjou**. They plotted to overthrow Edward IV and restore Henry VI. Warwick also gained the support of Edward's brother, George, Duke of Clarence, who had become estranged from the king, partly due to envy and discontent.

The Readeption of Henry VI (1470–1471)

Warwick's rebellion forced Edward IV to flee to Burgundy in October 1470. In a dramatic event called the **Readeption**, Henry VI was briefly reinstated as king under Warwick's guidance. However, Henry was a mere figurehead—physically frail and mentally fragile—while Warwick wielded real power.

Edward IV's Triumphant Return

In early 1471, Edward IV, backed by Burgundian funds, landed in England with a small force. Gaining followers as he advanced, Edward re-entered London almost unopposed. Henry VI fell back into Yorkist custody, while Warwick scrambled to assemble an army.

- **Battle of Barnet (April 1471)**: Edward IV met Warwick's forces near Barnet, north of London. A thick fog caused confusion, and both sides fired on their own troops at times. The Yorkists emerged victorious, and Warwick was killed while trying to flee.
- **Battle of Tewkesbury (May 1471)**: Margaret of Anjou, returning from France with Prince Edward, arrived too late to save Warwick. Edward IV pursued them, and at Tewkesbury, the Lancastrians suffered another crushing defeat. Prince Edward was killed, and Margaret was captured. Soon after, Henry VI was quietly murdered in the Tower of London—likely on Edward's orders—to eliminate any further Lancastrian challenge.

Edward IV now stood unchallenged. The Lancastrian lineage appeared extinguished with the deaths of Henry VI and his son.

Section VII: The End of Edward IV's Reign and the Rise of Richard III

Relative Peace (1471–1483)

For the next twelve years, England experienced relative stability. Edward IV ruled firmly, rewarding loyal supporters, maintaining profitable trade alliances, and continuing to develop a more structured royal administration. Though heavy taxation for war ended, Edward's court was not free from intrigues, as noble families jockeyed for influence.

Edward's Unexpected Death and the Succession Crisis

Edward IV died suddenly in April 1483, at only 40 years old, leaving two young sons: Edward (Prince of Wales) and Richard (Duke of York). Edward IV named his brother, Richard, Duke of Gloucester, as Lord Protector. However, factions within the Woodville family, including the boys' mother, Elizabeth Woodville, attempted to control the regency themselves.

Section VIII: Richard III's Controversial Ascendancy

The Princes in the Tower

Richard, Duke of Gloucester, moved swiftly. He arrested key Woodville supporters, including Elizabeth's brother and son by her first marriage. He took custody of the young King Edward V and his brother Richard, allegedly for their protection in the Tower of London. Within weeks, rumors spread that the princes had disappeared.

Claiming the Throne

Richard declared the princes illegitimate, claiming Edward IV's marriage to Elizabeth Woodville was invalid due to a pre-contract. Parliament accepted this argument under an act known as **Titulus Regius**, proclaiming Richard the rightful king. In July 1483, he was crowned **Richard III**. The whereabouts of the princes remained unknown; most believed they were quietly murdered, though the exact circumstances remain one of history's mysteries.

Early Revolts Against Richard III

Richard III's usurpation caused alarm among many nobles who had supported Edward IV's line. Disaffected Yorkists joined with Lancastrian sympathizers still resentful of past defeats. One notable figure was **Henry Tudor**, a distant Lancastrian claimant living in exile. With the princes presumed dead, Henry became a focus of opposition to Richard III.

Section IX: The Rise of the Tudor Dynasty

Henry Tudor's Claim

Henry Tudor descended from John of Gaunt (a son of Edward III) through an illegitimate branch later legitimized. His claim was weaker than others in a strict genealogical sense, but with most direct Lancastrians dead and the Yorkist line divided, Henry's cause gathered strength. He also promised to marry Elizabeth of York, the eldest daughter of Edward IV, thus uniting the two roses—red and white—and bringing peace to the realm.

Invasion and the Battle of Bosworth Field (1485)

In August 1485, Henry Tudor landed in Wales with French support. Marching east, he rallied Welsh and English lords unhappy with Richard III. The climactic battle occurred at **Bosworth Field**, near Leicester, on August 22, 1485.

- **Key Players**: Richard III commanded a royal force, while Henry Tudor's army was smaller but determined. Crucially, Thomas, Lord Stanley, and his brother Sir William Stanley, who had feigned loyalty to Richard, waited to see which side had the advantage before intervening.
- **Richard III's Death**: Early in the fight, Richard bravely charged toward Henry Tudor, hoping to end the conflict by killing him in single combat. The Stanleys suddenly switched sides, surrounding Richard. He was killed in the melee, and his crown was famously found and handed to Henry.

- **Aftermath**: Henry was proclaimed King Henry VII on the battlefield. He then married Elizabeth of York, symbolically uniting Lancaster and York. This marriage laid the foundation for the **Tudor dynasty**, which would rule England for over a century.

Section X: Final Skirmishes and Lasting Effects

The Battle of Stoke Field (1487)

Though Bosworth ended Richard III's reign, some Yorkist diehards attempted one more uprising. In 1487, they backed an impostor named Lambert Simnel (claiming to be Edward, Earl of Warwick) to challenge Henry VII. The rebels were defeated at **Stoke Field**, generally considered the last pitched battle of the Wars of the Roses. With this victory, Henry VII secured his throne more firmly.

Outcomes and Significance

1. **Monarchy Strengthened**: The Tudor regime reduced the power of over-mighty nobles. By limiting private armies (livery and maintenance) and asserting royal authority, Henry VII laid groundwork for a stronger centralized state.
2. **End of Plantagenet Rule**: The Plantagenet dynasty, which had ruled England since 1154, gave way to the Tudors. This shift concluded centuries of intermittent feudal turmoil.
3. **Symbolic Unity**: Henry VII's emblem, the **Tudor Rose**, combined the red rose of Lancaster and the white rose of York. Though the wars themselves were not strictly about "roses" in a romantic sense, this symbol represented the desire for unity after decades of strife.
4. **Socio-Economic Shifts**: Continuous civil war weakened many noble families, allowing new men—lawyers, administrators, lesser gentry—to rise in influence at court. This changing social landscape helped pave the way for new administrative and financial policies.
5. **Influence on Future Conflicts**: The Wars of the Roses demonstrated the dangers of ambiguous succession and the destructive potential of feuding nobles. Many subsequent monarchs, notably the Tudors, took pains to prevent similar dynastic crises.

Myth vs. Reality

The name "Wars of the Roses" was popularized later by historians and writers like William Shakespeare, who dramatized figures such as Richard III. The wars were not a single, continuous conflict but a series of rebellions, power grabs, and short battles. Nor were they purely symbolic of red and white roses—these badges evolved over time. Nonetheless, the image of two rival roses remains powerful in English cultural memory.

Chapter 11: The Ottoman Expansion and Conflicts in Eastern Europe

Introduction

In the late Middle Ages, a small Turkish principality rose to prominence in Anatolia (modern-day Turkey). This state—commonly known as the Ottoman Beylik—grew into one of the most powerful empires in history, the **Ottoman Empire**. Over several centuries, the Ottomans expanded into southeastern Europe, the Middle East, and North Africa, building a multi-ethnic, multi-religious empire. Their armies clashed repeatedly with the remnants of the Byzantine Empire, various Balkan principalities, the Kingdom of Hungary, the Polish-Lithuanian Commonwealth, and the Habsburg Monarchy—leading to countless wars that left a profound mark on Eastern Europe.

In this chapter, we will trace how the Ottoman Empire emerged and expanded, focusing on major conquests in Europe. We will explore the empire's political and military structures, examine key battles that reshaped frontiers, and discuss how local powers struggled to resist or accommodate this powerful new force. Finally, we will see how these conflicts influenced the future of Europe—altering political alliances, trade routes, and cultural identities in a region caught between East and West.

Section I: The Roots of the Ottoman State

The Decline of the Seljuks and the Rise of Osman

The Ottoman Empire owes its name to **Osman I**, a Turkish chieftain who led a small emirate in northwestern Anatolia around the turn of the 14th century. The region was fragmented following the decline of the Seljuk Sultanate of Rum, itself weakened by Mongol invasions. Various local Turkish warlords controlled pockets of land, yet none initially seemed poised to dominate. Osman's beylik was one among many, located near the frontiers of the weakening Byzantine Empire.

- **Gazi Warriors**: Osman and his followers identified themselves as **gazi** warriors, fighting in the name of Islam against non-Muslim neighbors. This sense of religious struggle helped attract volunteers and allies, creating a strong martial ethos that fueled expansion.
- **Strategic Location**: Situated close to Byzantine lands, Osman's realm constantly engaged in raids and small conquests. Over time, his successors inherited this strategic advantage.

Orhan and the First Footsteps into Europe

Osman's son, **Orhan (r. 1324–1362)**, continued to strengthen the Ottoman state. He expanded in Anatolia and began forging alliances through marriages and truces. Under Orhan, the Ottomans captured cities like Bursa, establishing a foothold in northwest Anatolia that would serve as a base for future growth.

- **Crossing the Dardanelles**: Around the mid-14th century, the Ottomans gained a bridgehead in Thrace (southeastern Europe) when Byzantine factions allowed Ottoman troops to cross into Europe as mercenaries or allies in internal Byzantine disputes. This move proved crucial, as the Ottomans then established permanent forts and settlements on European soil.

By Orhan's death, the Ottomans had transformed from a small border emirate into a rising regional power straddling two continents.

Section II: Early Conquests and the March into the Balkans

Murad I and the Creation of a Standing Army

Under **Sultan Murad I (r. 1362–1389)**, Ottoman expansion into the Balkans accelerated. Murad shifted the capital to Edirne (Adrianople) in Thrace, affirming that Europe—not just Anatolia—was essential to the empire's future.

- **Janissaries**: A groundbreaking military innovation under Murad was the development of the **Janissary corps**. These were elite infantry units

originally drawn from the **devshirme** system—Christian youths taken from conquered areas, converted to Islam, and trained as professional soldiers loyal to the sultan. Over time, the Janissaries became the backbone of Ottoman armies, feared for their discipline and skill with firearms.
- **Feudal Cavalry (Sipahi)**: Murad also relied on **sipahis**, cavalrymen who held fiefs (called **timars**) in exchange for military service. This arrangement tied local administrators and warriors to the sultan, strengthening centralized control.

Battles of Maritsa and Kosovo

- **Battle of Maritsa (1371)**: A coalition of Serbian and other Balkan lords advanced on the Ottomans but suffered a crushing defeat at the Maritsa River. Ottoman troops launched a surprise night attack, devastating the Balkan forces and signaling that the Ottoman threat could not be easily dismissed.
- **Battle of Kosovo (1389)**: Perhaps the most famous medieval Balkan conflict, Kosovo pitted Murad I against a broad Serbian-led coalition. The battle was fierce, and both Sultan Murad and Serbian leader Prince Lazar were killed. While the immediate outcome was not a complete Ottoman occupation, the morale effects were significant: Serbia became more vulnerable, and the mythic status of Kosovo shaped South Slavic consciousness for centuries.

By the late 14th century, the Ottomans had secured significant control over Bulgaria, parts of Macedonia, and other Balkan regions. Many local rulers paid tribute or became vassals, reducing open resistance.

Section III: Bayezid I and the Clash at Nicopolis

Sultan Bayezid I: Expansion and Ambition

Bayezid I (r. 1389–1402), known as "the Thunderbolt," inherited an expanding empire. He swiftly moved against remaining Balkan states and pressed the siege of Constantinople itself, seeking to capture the Byzantine capital. Although Constantinople did not fall during Bayezid's reign, his campaigns alarmed Western European powers, prompting them to intervene.

- **Nicopolis Crusade (1396)**: A large crusading army led by Hungarian King Sigismund, joined by French, Burgundian, and other European knights, marched to relieve the Balkans. At **Nicopolis** (in present-day Bulgaria), Bayezid's forces triumphed decisively. Overconfidence and disorganization among the crusaders contributed to the Ottoman victory. The defeat shocked Europe, solidifying the Ottomans' reputation as a formidable power.

The Timurid Invasion and Temporary Disruption

Just as Bayezid's armies threatened Eastern Europe, a new danger emerged from the east: the **Timurid Empire** under **Timur (Tamerlane)**. In 1402, Timur's forces crushed Bayezid at the **Battle of Ankara**, leading to Bayezid's capture and the temporary collapse of centralized Ottoman authority. This crisis, known as the **Ottoman Interregnum (1402–1413)**, halted Ottoman expansion in Europe for a decade. Princes in the Balkan vassal states took advantage of Ottoman infighting to regain some autonomy, but the empire soon recovered under Mehmed I and Murad II, who restored central control.

Section IV: The Fall of Constantinople and the Height of Expansion

Sultan Mchmed II ("the Conqueror")

Mehmed II (r. 1451–1481) is best known for capturing Constantinople in 1453, an event that ended the Byzantine Empire and resonated across Europe. Although not the only campaign of his reign, this victory confirmed the Ottomans as heirs to the Eastern Roman (Byzantine) legacy in many eyes, while terrifying Christian states.

- **Innovations in Siege Warfare**: Mehmed employed massive cannons, engineered by specialists like Orban, to batter Constantinople's famous walls. A carefully coordinated land-and-sea blockade sealed the city's fate.
- **Aftermath**: Renaming the city **Istanbul**, Mehmed II repopulated and revitalized it, making it the empire's capital. He also continued conquests in Serbia, Bosnia, and the Aegean, consolidating Ottoman control in southeastern Europe.

Balkan and Black Sea Campaigns

Mehmed II targeted the Despotate of Morea in the Peloponnese, subduing Greek states. He also extended Ottoman influence along the Black Sea coast, annexing the Genoese colonies in the Crimea and forging alliances with Tatar khans.

Legacy of Mehmed II

Dubbed "the Conqueror," Mehmed II's rule restructured the empire's administrative systems, centralizing authority. He balanced continuity with innovation, welcoming scholars and artists from conquered lands. Although much of Europe viewed him as a dangerous adversary, within the empire, Mehmed was lionized as a just, ambitious sultan who had fulfilled the dream of taking Constantinople.

Section V: Conflict with Hungary and the Habsburgs

The Reigns of Selim I and Suleiman the Magnificent

After Mehmed II, the empire saw leaders like **Selim I (r. 1512–1520)**, who focused on conquering the Mamluks in Syria and Egypt. Then came **Suleiman I (r. 1520–1566)**, often called **Suleiman the Magnificent** in the West and **Kanuni (the Lawgiver)** in the Islamic world. Suleiman expanded the empire further into Europe, capturing Belgrade in 1521 and turning to Hungary next.

- **Battle of Mohács (1526)**: One of the most significant Ottoman victories in Europe, Mohács saw the Hungarian army decisively defeated, and King Louis II was killed. The Hungarian Kingdom was left leaderless, enabling the Ottomans to occupy much of central Hungary and place a vassal on the throne of Transylvania.
- **First Siege of Vienna (1529)**: Suleiman pushed towards the Habsburg capital, Vienna. Despite logistical challenges and worsening weather, Ottoman troops reached the city's walls. However, supply shortages, disease, and stiff resistance forced a withdrawal. Although not a total defeat, Suleiman's failure to capture Vienna represented a symbolic limit to rapid Ottoman expansion deep into Central Europe.

Wars with the Habsburg Monarchy

Following Mohács, the Habsburgs claimed parts of Hungary, leading to a protracted struggle with the Ottomans. The region became a **military frontier**, with fortresses and garrisons along the Danube. Cities like Buda and Pest fell under Ottoman rule, while the Habsburgs held the western portion of Hungary. Skirmishes, sieges, and shifting alliances characterized this frontier zone for decades.

- **Long War (1593–1606)**: This was a major conflict between the Ottomans and the Habsburgs (and their allies), marked by brutal, back-and-forth campaigns in Hungary. Although neither side achieved a decisive victory, the war drained resources and tested the limits of the Ottoman military machine.

Section VI: Struggles on Multiple Fronts

Conflicts with Poland-Lithuania

The Ottoman Empire also clashed with the **Polish-Lithuanian Commonwealth**, a powerful state in Eastern Europe. While often overshadowed by Ottoman-Habsburg wars, these encounters included significant campaigns:

- **Moldavian Magnate Wars**: Moldavia, Wallachia, and Transylvania were vassal states or semi-independent principalities that frequently changed allegiance, causing friction between Poland-Lithuania and the Ottomans.
- **Battle of Cecora (1620)** and **Khotyn (1621)**: In these engagements, Polish-Lithuanian forces, including the famous winged hussars, confronted Ottoman armies and Tatar auxiliaries. While the Ottomans enjoyed some successes, the Poles held them at bay, illustrating the difficulty of subduing all of Eastern Europe.

Venetian Conflicts in the Mediterranean

The Ottoman navy, especially after acquiring shipyards and skilled sailors from conquered ports, challenged Venice and other maritime republics for control of the eastern Mediterranean. Key confrontations included:

- **Siege of Rhodes (1522)**: The Knights Hospitaller were expelled from the island by Suleiman's forces.
- **War of Cyprus (1570–1573)**: The Ottomans took Cyprus from Venice, but the Christian alliance known as the **Holy League** defeated the Ottoman fleet at the **Battle of Lepanto (1571)**. Although Lepanto did not end Ottoman naval power, it showed that the empire was not invincible at sea.

Section VII: The Seventeenth Century and the Second Siege of Vienna

Shifting Power Balances

By the mid-17th century, the Ottomans still held large parts of southeastern Europe, including much of Hungary, the Balkans, and the Aegean coasts. However, internal problems—court intrigues, economic strains, and the challenge of governing vast, diverse territories—affected their ability to expand further. Europe, too, was changing: stronger centralized states, better firearms, and improved fortifications made conquests more difficult.

- **Köprülü Viziers**: Under the leadership of the Köprülü family of grand viziers, the empire attempted reforms, revitalizing the military and bureaucracy in the late 17th century. This led to renewed offensives, targeting Habsburg lands again.

The Great Turkish War and Vienna (1683)

The **Great Turkish War (1683–1699)** saw a final major Ottoman push into Central Europe. Grand Vizier Kara Mustafa led a massive army to besiege Vienna for the second time in 1683. The city's defenses, aided by imperial and Polish reinforcements under King John III Sobieski, repelled the Ottomans. The **Battle of Vienna (September 12, 1683)** turned into a decisive defeat for the Ottomans, often seen as a turning point in Eastern European history.

- **Aftermath**: The Holy League (Austria, Poland-Lithuania, Venice, later joined by Russia) took the initiative, driving the Ottomans out of Hungary and part of the Balkans. The subsequent **Treaty of Karlowitz (1699)** forced the empire to cede significant territories, confirming a major territorial rollback in Europe.

Section VIII: Governance, Society, and Impact on Eastern Europe

Vassal States and Autonomy

The Ottomans often integrated conquered areas by leaving local rulers in place as vassals—especially in Wallachia, Moldavia, and Transylvania. These principalities paid tribute and provided military support but kept some internal autonomy. This flexible system allowed the empire to expand quickly without having to administer every region directly.

Religious Policies

While the Ottomans were a Muslim empire, they generally permitted Christian and Jewish communities to practice their faiths under the **millet system**. Each religious community had internal governance concerning personal law and religious practice, in return for loyalty and taxes to the sultan. This approach, more tolerant than some contemporary Christian kingdoms, helped maintain stability in multi-faith societies, though non-Muslims were subject to additional taxes and social restrictions.

Economic and Cultural Consequences

Ottoman control reoriented trade routes across the Balkans and the eastern Mediterranean. Constantinople (Istanbul) became a major commercial center, linking Europe and Asia. Local economies adapted to supply the Ottoman army, fueling both urban growth and rural exploitation. Architecturally, the Ottomans built mosques, bridges, and caravanserais that reshaped the urban landscapes of conquered cities.

- **Cultural Exchanges**: The empire's administrative class included officials fluent in multiple languages, reflecting the empire's diversity. Artistic and intellectual exchanges occurred between the Islamic world and Eastern Europe, influencing architecture, music, cuisine, and more. Over centuries, a distinctive Ottoman-Balkan cultural blend emerged.

Section IX: Key Battles and Their Significance

1. **Nicopolis (1396)**: Confirmed the Ottomans as the dominant force in the Balkans, humbling a Western crusade.
2. **Varna (1444)**: Another major victory over a crusading force, solidifying Ottoman hold on southeastern Europe.
3. **Constantinople (1453)**: Ended the Byzantine Empire and made Istanbul the Ottoman capital, symbolic of a new era.
4. **Mohács (1526)**: Crushed Hungarian independence, opening central Europe to Ottoman penetration.
5. **First Siege of Vienna (1529)**: Marked the high-water mark of Ottoman expansion into central Europe.
6. **Lepanto (1571)**: A significant naval defeat for the Ottomans at Christian hands, proving Ottoman fleets could be challenged.
7. **Second Siege of Vienna (1683)**: A turning point that led to the empire's gradual retreat from Hungary and parts of the Balkans.

Chapter 12: The Thirty Years' War

Introduction

From 1618 to 1648, the **Holy Roman Empire** and much of Europe were engulfed in one of the most devastating conflicts in the continent's history: the **Thirty Years' War**. Initially sparked by religious disputes between Catholics and Protestants, the war expanded into a complex political struggle involving multiple powers—Austria, Spain, France, Sweden, Denmark, the Dutch Republic, and numerous German principalities. Entire regions were laid to waste, populations were uprooted, and economies shattered.

In this chapter, we will explore the causes, key phases, and major figures of the Thirty Years' War. We will see how evolving alliances, shifting objectives, and the interplay of religious fervor and state ambition prolonged the war. Finally, we will discuss the **Peace of Westphalia (1648)**—a watershed treaty that influenced the future of diplomacy and the modern concept of sovereign states.

Section I: Background and Causes

The Holy Roman Empire and Religious Tensions

By the early 17th century, the Holy Roman Empire was a patchwork of hundreds of states—duchies, principalities, free cities—nominally under the emperor's authority. The Reformation in the 16th century had deepened divisions: some states embraced Lutheranism or Calvinism, others remained Catholic. While the **Peace of Augsburg (1555)** had allowed for a temporary settlement between Catholics and Lutherans, it excluded Calvinists and did not resolve the underlying tension of whether rulers or subjects could determine a territory's faith.

- **Habsburg Dominance**: The emperors from the House of Habsburg (based in Austria) aimed to strengthen Catholicism and centralize power. Many Protestant princes resisted, fearing the loss of autonomy.

- **Imperial Courts and Diets**: Rulers convened in imperial assemblies, but compromise was fragile. Any perceived violation of religious balance could spark conflict.

The Bohemian Situation

The Kingdom of Bohemia (modern-day Czech Republic) was part of the Holy Roman Empire. Its nobility included both Protestants and Catholics, but the Habsburg kings, as rulers of Bohemia, leaned toward Catholic policies.

- **Letter of Majesty (1609)**: Emperor Rudolph II had granted Bohemian Protestants certain freedoms of worship. When Emperor Ferdinand II (a staunch Catholic) sought to curtail these liberties, Bohemian nobles grew alarmed.
- **Defenestration of Prague (1618)**: On May 23, 1618, Protestant nobles threw two royal Catholic regents out of a window in Prague Castle. They survived the fall, but the incident became a symbolic spark for open revolt.

This revolt in Bohemia is commonly cited as the starting point of the Thirty Years' War.

Section II: Phase One — The Bohemian Revolt (1618–1625)

The Battle of White Mountain

Bohemian rebels formed a provisional government, declared Ferdinand II deposed in Bohemia, and offered the crown to **Frederick V**, the Protestant Elector Palatine (nicknamed the "Winter King"). Ferdinand, however, mustered Imperial and Spanish Habsburg support.

- **Battle of White Mountain (1620)**: Near Prague, the imperial forces crushed the Bohemian army. The rebellion collapsed swiftly; Frederick V fled, earning ridicule for his brief rule. Imperial forces imposed harsh penalties on Bohemian Protestants. Lands were confiscated, and Catholic power was entrenched.

Consequences for the Palatinate

Frederick V also lost his hereditary lands in the Rhineland, the **Palatinate**, which were occupied by Spanish and Bavarian troops. This alarmed other Protestant princes and powers like England (whose king, James I, was Frederick's father-in-law). Though they did not immediately intervene with large armies, distrust of the Habsburg design increased.

Section III: Phase Two — The Danish Intervention (1625–1629)

Christian IV of Denmark Enters the War

Christian IV, the Lutheran king of Denmark and Norway, feared rising Habsburg influence in the Protestant German states. Encouraged by England and the Dutch Republic (both eager to curb Habsburg power), Christian IV invaded northern Germany in 1625, hoping to protect Protestant interests and expand Danish control.

- **Imperial Response**: Emperor Ferdinand II enlisted **Albrecht von Wallenstein**, a Bohemian noble who raised a large private army loyal to the emperor. Another imperial commander, **Johann Tserclaes, Count of Tilly**, led the Catholic League's forces. Together, they pushed back Christian IV.

Defeat of Denmark

By 1626–1627, the Danish armies suffered defeats at **Lutter** and elsewhere. Wallenstein's forces occupied much of northern Germany, ravaging Protestant lands. Christian IV retreated, eventually seeking peace.

- **Treaty of Lübeck (1629)**: Denmark withdrew from the war in exchange for the return of its occupied territories. However, Denmark's influence in German affairs waned. The imperial-Catholic side appeared dominant, fueling a new wave of Catholic assertiveness.

Edict of Restitution

In 1629, emboldened by victories, Ferdinand II issued the **Edict of Restitution**, demanding that all Church lands secularized by Protestants since 1552 be returned to the Catholic Church. This threatened numerous Lutheran and Calvinist princes who had taken over former monastic or bishopric estates. Tensions soared; many Protestant states feared losing wealth and independence.

Section IV: Phase Three — Swedish Intervention (1630–1635)

The Rise of Gustavus Adolphus

Sweden, under **King Gustavus Adolphus** (r. 1611–1632), was emerging as a major Baltic power. Gustavus was a devout Lutheran who viewed Ferdinand II's policies as a threat to Protestant liberties. Moreover, Sweden had strategic reasons to curb Habsburg expansion that could endanger Swedish interests in the Baltic region.

- **Swedish Landing (1630)**: In July 1630, Gustavus Adolphus landed in northern Germany with a well-trained, modern army. He introduced more flexible tactics, including smaller infantry brigades, standardized artillery, and disciplined cavalry charges.

Protestant Resurgence

Initially, some German Protestant princes hesitated to join Gustavus Adolphus, fearing imperial reprisal. But as the Swedish king won victories and showed discipline (limiting plundering of local populations), support increased. Gustavus negotiated alliances, securing finances from France. Yes, **France**—a Catholic kingdom under Cardinal Richelieu—secretly supported the Swedish Lutheran cause to weaken the Habsburgs.

- **Battle of Breitenfeld (1631)**: A turning point in the war. Gustavus Adolphus, allied with the Saxons, decisively defeated Tilly's Catholic League army near Leipzig. Swedish artillery and flexible formations

overwhelmed the larger imperial force. This victory electrified Protestant Europe and shattered the myth of Catholic invincibility.
- **Wallenstein's Return**: Emperor Ferdinand, alarmed by Tilly's defeats, recalled Wallenstein. He raised another massive army, clashed with Gustavus in several campaigns, and forced the Swedish king to fight more cautiously.

The Death of Gustavus Adolphus

- **Battle of Lützen (1632)**: Gustavus Adolphus secured another victory over Wallenstein, but the king himself was killed during the battle. His death was a major blow to the Swedish cause. Despite winning at Lützen, the leaderless Swedish armies struggled to maintain momentum afterward.

Peace Attempts and Continued Conflict

After Lützen, Swedish forces remained in Germany under Chancellor Oxenstierna's leadership, but internal divisions hampered coordination. Emperor Ferdinand II sought negotiations, yet the war dragged on. Wallenstein himself fell out of favor with the emperor, was accused of conspiracy, and was assassinated in 1634—removing another major player.

- **Battle of Nördlingen (1634)**: A crushing defeat for the Swedish-Protestant side at the hands of imperial and Spanish forces. The fiasco at Nördlingen led many German Protestant states to reconsider loyalty to Sweden and sign the **Peace of Prague (1635)**, which modified the Edict of Restitution but retained Habsburg authority. However, not all parties joined this peace, ensuring the war continued.

Section V: Phase Four — The French Intervention (1635–1648)

Cardinal Richelieu's Strategy

For France, the war was less about religion and more about **balance of power**. Surrounded by Habsburg territories (Spain to the south, the Holy Roman Empire to the east), France under **Cardinal Richelieu** wanted to curb Habsburg influence. Although France had funded Protestant armies indirectly, in 1635 it entered the war directly—allying with the Dutch Republic and some German princes.

- **War on Multiple Fronts**: France fought Spain along the Pyrenees and in the Spanish Netherlands, while also confronting imperial forces in southwestern Germany.

Prolonged Devastation in Germany

As the war raged, shifting alliances turned German principalities into battlegrounds. Armies on both sides lived off the land, pillaging towns and farms, causing widespread starvation and epidemic diseases. Historians estimate that parts of Germany lost up to one-third of their population, making the Thirty Years' War among the deadliest European conflicts prior to the 20th century.

- **Mercenary Armies**: Commanders recruited diverse soldiers—Germans, Swedes, Scots, French, Spaniards, Czechs, and others—often under mercenary captains who sold their services to the highest bidder. This environment fueled chaos, as discipline deteriorated and violence against civilians soared.

Key Engagements and Shifting Frontiers

- **Battle of Rocroi (1643)**: In the Spanish Netherlands, a French army led by the young Duke d'Enghien (later known as the Great Condé) crushed the renowned Spanish tercios, signaling the decline of Spain's old military supremacy.
- **Tussles Around the Rhine**: Control of the Rhine corridor was vital for trade and troop movements. Various sieges and battles ensued, each side temporarily seizing strategic fortresses.

By the mid-1640s, exhaustion set in. Spain's finances were crumbling, the Emperor faced ongoing rebellions, and France also felt the strain of continuous warfare. The impetus for a comprehensive peace grew stronger.

Section VI: The Peace of Westphalia (1648)

Negotiations in Münster and Osnabrück

Peace talks had begun as early as the 1630s in different locations, but the decisive negotiations took place in the Westphalian towns of **Münster** and **Osnabrück**, with countless delegations representing states both large and small. The complexity of the conflict required a grand diplomatic effort:

- **Multiple Parties**: The Holy Roman Emperor, France, Spain, Sweden, the Dutch Republic, various German princes, and lesser states each had demands and grievances.
- **Religious Compromises**: Recognizing the stalemate, Catholics, Lutherans, and Calvinists conceded mutual existence. The principle of **cuius regio, eius religio** (from the Peace of Augsburg) was reaffirmed, expanded to include Calvinists, and further clarified.

Main Provisions

1. **Territorial Adjustments:** Sweden gained territories in northern Germany (e.g., Pomerania), securing control over Baltic trade routes. France took parts of Alsace and confirmed rights in western Germany. Various principalities regained or lost lands as per new boundaries.
2. **Sovereign States:** Each German prince effectively gained the right to conduct foreign policy independently, weakening the emperor's centralized authority. The Holy Roman Empire thus remained fragmented, a loose confederation of sovereign entities.
3. **Religious Settlements:** The Peace of Westphalia ended major religious wars in the empire by giving legal recognition to Catholicism, Lutheranism, and Calvinism. Rulers could choose their realm's faith, but subjects had limited rights to practice privately if it differed from the official religion.

Impact and Significance

The Peace of Westphalia is often cited as the birth of the modern international system, where states recognized each other's sovereignty and strove for a balance of power rather than universal monarchy. Though the concept of sovereignty evolved further over time, Westphalia marked a milestone in diplomatic history:

- **France as a Great Power**: Weakened Habsburg influence allowed France to emerge as Europe's leading continental power, soon under the reign of Louis XIV.
- **Swedish Dominance in the North**: Sweden became a major Baltic power, though it would lose that status in later conflicts.
- **German Fragmentation**: The empire remained politically divided until the 19th century. The war's devastation slowed economic and social progress in many German states.

Section VII: War's Effects on Population and Society

Demographic Catastrophe

The Thirty Years' War wrought massive suffering for civilian populations. Chronic marauding, sieges, forced requisitions, and disease outbreaks led to famine and high mortality rates. Some cities shrank dramatically, while rural regions were left deserted.

- **Plague and Disease**: Armies crisscrossing Europe spread diseases such as the bubonic plague and typhus. Makeshift hospitals were overwhelmed, and entire villages disappeared.
- **Migration**: Thousands fled war zones for safer territories or emigrated to other parts of Europe. This population dislocation altered local economies, labor markets, and cultural landscapes.

Social and Economic Disruption

Farmers lost livestock and harvests, artisans lost markets, and trade routes were often cut off. Noble families scrambled to maintain incomes, sometimes turning to private war-bands or alliances with foreign powers. For many peasants, the war represented a near-constant state of upheaval, with taxes levied by whichever army controlled the region at the time.

Cultural Responses

Writers, artists, and chroniclers of the period recorded the war's horrors. In German-speaking lands, works like **Simplicius Simplicissimus** by Hans Jakob

Christoffel von Grimmelshausen vividly depicted the chaos of soldier life and peasant suffering. Religious art took on themes of suffering and redemption, reflecting the profound trauma of the era.

Section VIII: Key Military and Political Lessons

1. **Transition in Warfare**: Armies moved from feudal levies to professional or semi-professional forces reliant on firearms and artillery. Commanders like Gustavus Adolphus refined tactics that influenced European armies for generations.
2. **Diplomatic Complexity**: The war highlighted how religious, dynastic, and strategic considerations could intertwine in European politics. Powers would form alliances across confessional lines if it served their interests.
3. **Decentralization vs. Centralization**: The emperor's attempt to solidify Habsburg control met with fierce resistance from local states. The Peace of Westphalia confirmed the empire's decentralized nature, giving local rulers wide autonomy.
4. **Religion No Longer an Absolute Divider**: Although the war began with strong confessional motivations, by its end, political calculations often trumped religious loyalty (e.g., Catholic France supporting Protestant Sweden). This shift foreshadowed a Europe less driven by religious uniformity and more by state interest.

Chapter 13: The Wars of Louis XIV and Shifting European Alliances

Introduction

By the mid-17th century, France had emerged as one of the most powerful states in Europe. The Peace of Westphalia (1648) ended the Thirty Years' War, weakening the Habsburgs and allowing France to expand its influence. Soon after, Louis XIV—often called the **Sun King**—ascended the French throne. Ruling from 1643 to 1715 (with his personal rule beginning in 1661 after the death of Cardinal Mazarin), Louis XIV built a centralized state, reformed the army, and sought glory through warfare and territorial gains. His ambitions drew in other European powers fearful of French dominance, leading to a series of conflicts that reshaped alliances and the balance of power.

In this chapter, we will explore the major wars of Louis XIV, including the War of Devolution, the Dutch War, the War of the League of Augsburg (also known as the Nine Years' War), and the War of the Spanish Succession. We will examine how these conflicts were driven not only by Louis XIV's drive for prestige and expansion but also by the shifting alliances that formed to contain his power. Lastly, we will consider how these wars influenced the development of modern state systems and the ideas of balance-of-power diplomacy.

Section I: France's Position and Louis XIV's Ambition

The Aftermath of the Thirty Years' War

The Peace of Westphalia granted the French greater influence in German affairs, as Habsburg authority in the Holy Roman Empire weakened. France gained territories such as portions of Alsace, and French diplomacy targeted German princes to create friendly buffer states along France's eastern border. Internally, Cardinal Mazarin (who served as the chief minister to Louis XIV's mother, Anne of Austria) consolidated royal power by suppressing the Fronde (a series of civil wars from 1648 to 1653). By the time Louis XIV assumed full personal control at the age of twenty-three, the monarchy was stronger than ever.

The Centralized French State and Military Reforms

Louis XIV believed in the divine right of kings, centralizing administration in Versailles. He reduced the autonomy of provincial nobles, instituted a professional bureaucracy, and sponsored economic policies to enrich the state. A key figure in these reforms was **Jean-Baptiste Colbert**, Louis's finance minister, who promoted mercantilism, built up manufacturing, and supported naval expansion.

Perhaps most crucially, Louis XIV modernized the French army. **Michel Le Tellier** and later **François-Michel le Tellier, Marquis de Louvois** introduced regular drilling, standardized weapons, improved logistics, and quartermaster systems. This made the French military one of the most formidable forces in Europe. Louis's desire for military glory coupled with a powerful, well-funded army set the stage for a series of expansionist wars.

Section II: The War of Devolution (1667–1668)

Causes and Pretext

Louis XIV's first major conflict was the **War of Devolution** (1667–1668), in which he claimed Spanish Netherlands (roughly modern-day Belgium) for his wife, Maria Theresa of Spain. According to a local custom called "devolution," daughters of a first marriage could inherit territories if they were from certain provinces. Louis argued that Maria Theresa's Spanish dowry had not been paid, so the Spanish Netherlands rightfully "devolved" to France. Though the legal basis was questionable, Louis used it as a justification for invasion.

At this time, Spain was weakened after decades of conflict (including the Eighty Years' War with the Dutch and the long struggle in the Thirty Years' War). Sensing an opportunity, French troops quickly overran much of the Spanish Netherlands and Franche-Comté. Louis's rapid success alarmed neighboring states, including the Dutch Republic, England, and Sweden, which eventually formed a **Triple Alliance** to check French gains.

Key Campaigns and the Triple Alliance

In 1667, France's reorganized army performed efficiently, capturing fortresses like Charleroi, Tournai, and Lille. Louis's famed military engineer, **Sébastien Le Prestre de Vauban**, began a career of designing and upgrading fortifications that would make French strongholds nearly impregnable. Spain's forces were no match for the disciplined French army, and the Spanish Habsburg monarchy could not mount a robust defense.

However, the Dutch grew uneasy. They feared that if France dominated the Spanish Netherlands, the Dutch Republic would be threatened directly. England (then under Charles II) and Sweden also saw the need to prevent one state from becoming too powerful. Under diplomatic pressure from the **Triple Alliance**, Louis XIV agreed to negotiate rather than risk a wider war.

The Peace of Aix-la-Chapelle (1668)

The conflict ended with the **Treaty of Aix-la-Chapelle (1668)**. France kept some conquered towns in the Spanish Netherlands—most notably Lille—but returned Franche-Comté to Spain. Although this was a short war, the War of Devolution revealed two important trends: (1) France's growing military prowess and ambition under Louis XIV, and (2) the formation of anti-French alliances that would become a recurring pattern in European diplomacy.

Section III: The Dutch War (1672–1678)

Prelude: Tensions with the Dutch Republic

Despite the Triple Alliance, the Dutch had been Louis XIV's erstwhile allies during the Thirty Years' War. But the War of Devolution frayed trust. Louis XIV also resented the Dutch for blocking his designs in the Spanish Netherlands and for perceived slights to his prestige. Furthermore, French mercantilist policies clashed with the Dutch trading empire, heightening economic and commercial rivalry.

Louis sought to isolate the Dutch diplomatically. By negotiating with England, he tempted Charles II with subsidies and the promise of shared spoils. Sweden, often short on funds, could be swayed by French gold. Meanwhile, many German princes were open to French influence or bribes. With these maneuvers, Louis managed to dissolve or undermine the Triple Alliance, leaving the Dutch Republic more vulnerable.

The Invasion of the Dutch Republic (1672)

In 1672, French armies crossed the Rhine and advanced rapidly into Dutch territory. The French were joined by English forces, and initially the Dutch defenses collapsed under the weight of the surprise offensive. The heart of the Republic lay open to French occupation. The crisis led to a political revolution in the Netherlands: the powerful De Witt brothers were overthrown, and **William of Orange** was elevated as Stadtholder. He would become the main leader of Dutch resistance.

Facing catastrophic defeat, the Dutch resorted to opening the dikes—the so-called "Water Line"—flooding large areas to halt French armies. This drastic measure succeeded, preventing the fall of key Dutch cities like Amsterdam. Meanwhile, William of Orange skillfully built a new coalition. The Holy Roman Emperor Leopold I, Brandenburg-Prussia, and eventually Spain joined the war to curtail French advances.

Expansion of the Conflict and Key Battles

By 1673, the Dutch War turned into a broader European contest. The French, fighting across multiple fronts (Spanish Netherlands, Alsace, the Rhine, and Catalonia), still enjoyed initial successes, but the alliance against them grew stronger.

- **Siege Warfare**: Vauban's skillful engineering and fortress-building played a critical role. The French captured towns such as Maastricht (1673), but each siege took time and resources. The Dutch excelled at defensive operations with their water defenses.
- **Naval Engagements**: While overshadowed by land battles, the Anglo-French alliance initially challenged the Dutch navy at sea. However, famous Dutch admirals like Michiel de Ruyter fought the English in the North Sea and the Mediterranean, stymying full French naval domination. Eventually, England withdrew from the war in 1674 due to domestic political considerations and heavy costs.

The Peace of Nijmegen (1678–1679)

Years of costly fighting led to war-weariness on all sides. France had conquered parts of the Spanish Netherlands and some territories in Franche-Comté, but fully subduing the Dutch proved impossible. The war ended with the **Treaties of Nijmegen (1678–1679)**. The Dutch retained their independence, though they granted France some commercial concessions. Spain ceded Franche-Comté to France, along with key fortresses in the Spanish Netherlands.

This outcome showcased France's power. Despite not crushing the Dutch, Louis XIV had expanded French borders significantly—particularly by gaining complete control of Franche-Comté. Yet the rest of Europe saw that coalition warfare could limit French ambitions. Meanwhile, the conflict deepened the rivalry between Louis XIV and William of Orange, who would meet again in future wars.

Section IV: The War of the League of Augsburg (Nine Years' War, 1688–1697)

The "Reunions" and Growing Resistance

After the Dutch War, Louis XIV turned to diplomatic means to consolidate and expand French territory. Using special courts called "Chambers of Reunion," France claimed overlapping jurisdictions and historical rights to various border towns in the Holy Roman Empire. Fortresses such as Strasbourg fell under French control. Although these were mostly bloodless takeovers, they alarmed German princes, the Dutch, and even England, which was now ruled by William of Orange as **William III** (following the Glorious Revolution of 1688).

Tensions spiked when Louis revoked the **Edict of Nantes** in 1685, ending legal toleration for French Protestants (Huguenots). This move alienated Protestant states, eroding any sympathy they might have had for France. As Louis extended his fortifications along the Rhine and threatened the Palatinate, a broad anti-French coalition began to form.

Outbreak of War: The League of Augsburg

In 1688, France invaded the Rhineland, expecting a short conflict to secure more forward defenses. However, the response was swift. Emperor Leopold I, various German princes, Spain, Sweden, and the Dutch Republic united in the **League of Augsburg** (later called the Grand Alliance when England joined). William III of Orange, now King of England, brought English financial and naval power into the alliance against Louis XIV.

Major Theaters of the Nine Years' War

1. **The Rhineland and the Palatinate**: French forces scorched parts of the Palatinate, demolishing towns to create a buffer zone. This tactic generated considerable outrage across Europe.
2. **The Low Countries**: Repeated campaigns saw French and Allied armies maneuver in the Spanish Netherlands (modern Belgium). Vauban's fortresses made direct assaults expensive, so the war devolved into sieges and positional battles.
3. **Naval Conflicts**: At sea, the Anglo-Dutch fleets faced the French navy in the Atlantic and Mediterranean. Although the French navy was formidable initially, it struggled against the combined maritime might of the Dutch and English over time.
4. **Irish Campaign**: The war intersected with the **Williamite War in Ireland** (1689–1691), where King James II (deposed by the Glorious Revolution) and French forces tried to reclaim the English throne through Ireland. William III ultimately defeated them at battles like the Boyne (1690) and Aughrim (1691).

Economic Warfare and the Strain on France

By the mid-1690s, both sides were exhausted. France faced severe economic shortages, crop failures, and heavy taxation. The Allies also bore the burden of prolonged fighting. Diplomacy edged toward compromise. The war ended with the **Peace of Ryswick (1697)**, where Louis XIV recognized William III as the legitimate King of England and restored some territories to various German states. France retained parts of Alsace and other gains, but the ambition for further expansion receded, at least temporarily.

The Nine Years' War was arguably Europe's first major conflict fought on multiple continents. France and England clashed in colonial outposts in the Americas and Asia, hinting at the future shape of global warfare. But its primary significance lay in reinforcing the concept of a European balance of power and the willingness of states to form grand alliances to check one dominant state.

Section V: The War of the Spanish Succession (1701–1714)

The Succession Crisis in Spain

The final—and arguably most significant—war of Louis XIV's reign centered on the Spanish throne. The aging, childless King Charles II of Spain (the last Habsburg ruler there) had a vast empire spanning Spain, Spanish Netherlands, parts of Italy, and overseas colonies. Charles II's eventual successor would tilt Europe's balance of power dramatically. Both the Habsburgs (in Austria) and the Bourbons (in France) had dynastic claims. Other powers dreaded either outcome, fearing an oversized Austrian or French empire.

In 1700, Charles II died and willed his entire inheritance to **Philip of Anjou**, Louis XIV's grandson. If France and Spain united under Bourbon rule, this might create a superstate overshadowing Europe. Louis XIV accepted the will, proclaiming Philip as Philip V of Spain. Outraged, England, the Dutch Republic, the Holy Roman Emperor (Leopold I, and later Joseph I), and other states formed another **Grand Alliance** to prevent Bourbon dominance.

Early Battles and Shifting Fronts

The **War of the Spanish Succession** erupted in 1701. Major fronts included:

1. **Spanish Netherlands / Low Countries**: A crucial zone where Allied armies, led by England's Duke of Marlborough (John Churchill) and the Dutch commander Anthonie Heinsius, faced French marshals.
2. **Upper Rhine / Germany**: Imperial forces battled French armies along the Rhine.

3. **Italy**: Particularly in northern Italy (the Duchies of Milan and Mantua), where Austrian Habsburg claims collided with French interests. The Duke of Savoy initially sided with France but switched alliances to the Austrians.
4. **Spain Itself**: Different regions of Spain backed either Philip V (Bourbon) or Archduke Charles of Austria (the Habsburg claimant). Catalonia, for example, largely supported the Habsburg cause.

The Great Commanders: Marlborough and Prince Eugene

Two remarkable Allied generals shaped much of the war's course:

- **John Churchill, 1st Duke of Marlborough (England)**: A brilliant tactician and strategist, he led decisive campaigns. Famous battles included Blenheim (1704), Ramillies (1706), Oudenarde (1708), and Malplaquet (1709). These victories severely eroded French power in the Low Countries and southern Germany.
- **Prince Eugene of Savoy (Austria)**: A skillful commander who cooperated effectively with Marlborough. His victories against the French in Italy and with Marlborough in Germany were critical to the Allied cause.

France Under Siege

By 1708–1709, Allied armies had penetrated deep into northern France. Louis XIV's finances were strained, harvests failed, and popular discontent rose. Yet the French monarchy did not collapse. Instead, the Allies faced their own strains, as the war dragged on and casualties mounted. The **Battle of Malplaquet** (1709), despite being a narrow Allied success, was extraordinarily bloody, tempering the Allies' resolve to push deeper into France.

Diplomatic Shifts and the Peace Treaties

A major turning point occurred in 1711 when Emperor Joseph I died, leaving the Austrian throne to his brother, Archduke Charles—who was also the Habsburg claimant to Spain. If Charles gained both Austria and Spain, that union might be just as threatening as a Franco-Spanish Bourbon axis. England and the Dutch Republic grew wary of continuing the war for the sake of Habsburg aggrandizement. Negotiations advanced.

- **Treaty of Utrecht (1713)**: England, the Dutch, and other allies reached terms with France. Philip V was recognized as King of Spain but was barred from inheriting the French throne, preventing a total Bourbon merger. Spain's European territories in the Netherlands and Italy were partitioned among the Allies: Austria gained Milan, Naples, and the Spanish Netherlands (renamed Austrian Netherlands), while Savoy gained Sicily (later swapped for Sardinia). England gained Gibraltar and Minorca, strategic positions in the Mediterranean, plus trading privileges (such as the Asiento to supply slaves to Spanish colonies).
- **Treaties of Rastatt and Baden (1714)**: The Holy Roman Emperor agreed to similar terms, ending the war in the empire.

The War of the Spanish Succession concluded with a new balance of power. The Bourbons kept Spain, but France's expansionist momentum was curbed. Meanwhile, Great Britain (formed by the 1707 union of England and Scotland) emerged as a major maritime and commercial power, Austria consolidated its holdings in Italy and the Netherlands, and the Dutch Republic preserved independence but began to decline relative to Britain and France.

Section VI: Impact on European Warfare and Diplomacy

Professional Armies and Logistics

Louis XIV's wars, stretching over decades, solidified the practice of maintaining large standing armies. Logistics, supply lines, and fortifications became more sophisticated. Commanders like Marlborough and Prince Eugene refined combined-arms tactics, coordinating infantry, cavalry, and artillery. Sieges remained a critical element, but open battles like Blenheim or Ramillies showed the value of offensive maneuver and disciplined firepower.

Rise of the Balance-of-Power System

Repeated anti-French coalitions demonstrated the European preference for **balance-of-power** politics. Nations joined forces to block any single state's dominance. This approach guided diplomacy for much of the 18th century, leading to alliances that sometimes cut across religious or dynastic lines. The War of the Spanish Succession, in particular, was resolved as much by negotiations among allies as by victories on the battlefield.

Socio-Economic Strains

Decades of warfare imposed huge fiscal and human costs. France under Louis XIV introduced new taxes, sold offices, and borrowed heavily. Peasants in frontier regions endured repeated invasions, sieges, and pillaging. The Allied states also faced rising debts. The wars spurred innovations in public finance, including the development of government bonds, central banks (as in England), and more complex taxation systems.

Cultural Influence

Louis XIV's court culture at Versailles spread French language and fashions across Europe, even as foreign powers fought his armies. Diplomats adopted French as a common language, aristocrats imitated French court rituals, and architects drew inspiration from French baroque designs. Ironically, the more Louis's wars antagonized his neighbors, the more French culture, in some respects, gained prestige.

Section VII: The Sunset of Louis XIV's Reign

When the War of the Spanish Succession ended in 1714, France was exhausted—laden with debt, mourning high casualties, and facing a generation of hostility from neighboring states. Louis XIV died in 1715, leaving the throne to his five-year-old great-grandson, Louis XV. Historians debate whether Louis XIV's wars left France stronger or weaker overall. Undoubtedly, France retained an impressive military apparatus and significant territorial gains (e.g., Alsace, Franche-Comté), but its resources were strained, and it had created a lasting coalition of rival powers poised to check future French ambitions.

His reign remains a defining period in European history, symbolizing both the grandeur of absolutist monarchy and the catastrophic possibilities of near-constant warfare. Diplomatically, the period set the pattern for the 18th century: complex alliances shifting to maintain equilibrium. Militarily, it showcased the evolution from pike-and-shot armies to more uniform, disciplined troops, supported by state bureaucracy. Socially, it highlighted the burdens of mercantilism and taxation needed to sustain a permanent war footing.

Chapter 14: The Seven Years' War

Introduction

By the mid-18th century, Europe had undergone multiple realignments since the days of Louis XIV. The War of the Austrian Succession (1740–1748) had reshuffled alliances and left many questions unresolved, particularly regarding the balance of power in Central Europe and overseas colonies. Rising tensions between Great Britain and France over colonial expansion and trade sharpened across the globe. Meanwhile, in Central Europe, Prussia under Frederick II (later called Frederick the Great) had emerged as a formidable kingdom, challenging Habsburg Austria for dominance in the German-speaking world.

These intertwined rivalries erupted into the **Seven Years' War (1756–1763)**, a global conflict often dubbed the first true "world war." It pitted two main coalitions: Britain and Prussia on one side, and France, Austria, Russia, and others on the other. Battles raged in Europe, North America, India, West Africa, and the Caribbean, with far-reaching consequences for colonial empires, state finances, and the geopolitical map. This chapter examines the causes, principal theaters, major campaigns, and outcomes of the Seven Years' War—an event that reshaped the modern world and set the stage for future revolutions.

Section I: Shifting Alliances and the Diplomatic Revolution

Aftermath of the War of the Austrian Succession

The War of the Austrian Succession ended with the **Treaty of Aix-la-Chapelle (1748)**. Maria Theresa of Austria had managed to keep her domains largely intact, but Prussia retained Silesia—a rich province seized by Frederick II. France, allied with Prussia during that conflict, gained little, while Britain had supported Austria but became increasingly focused on colonial competition with France.

The 1748 peace left Austria determined to recover Silesia, while Prussia aimed to keep it. Great Britain and France eyed each other across continents: North

America, where the British colonies clashed with French Canada; India, where trading companies vied for local alliances; and the Caribbean, where sugar islands generated massive wealth.

The Diplomatic Revolution (1756)

Traditionally, Habsburg Austria was allied with Britain against France. But alarmed by Prussia's strength, Austria's foreign minister, **Wenzel Anton Kaunitz**, orchestrated a surprising shift: Austria formed an alliance with its old rival, France. Meanwhile, Britain—fearing French power at sea—aligned with Prussia. Russia, seeing Prussia's rise as a threat in Eastern Europe, joined Austria and France. Sweden also leaned toward the Franco-Austrian side. This sudden realignment was termed the **Diplomatic Revolution** of 1756.

As tensions rose, Frederick II preemptively struck Saxony, a smaller German state allied with Austria, starting a new war on the European continent. Soon, the conflict extended worldwide due to colonial rivalries between Britain and France, merging into the grand confrontation now known as the Seven Years' War.

Section II: European Theater – The Struggle for Continental Supremacy

Prussia vs. Austria, France, and Russia

At the war's outset, Prussia faced the daunting prospect of fighting multiple great powers simultaneously. Frederick II hoped his disciplined army and swift maneuvers could offset numerical inferiority. He enjoyed financial and some naval support from Britain, which recognized that defending Hanover (a British possession in Germany) was tied to Prussian success on land.

1. **Invasion of Saxony (1756)**: Frederick's rapid incursion forced the Saxon army to surrender at Pirna. This action alarmed Europe and solidified the Austro-French-Russian coalition.
2. **Battle of Lobositz (1756)**: A near stalemate but allowed Frederick to maintain momentum.

3. **Early Triumphs and Setbacks**: In 1757, Frederick won notable victories at Rossbach (against the French and Imperial army) and Leuthen (against the Austrians). These successes became legendary, showcasing the agility of Prussian infantry and Frederick's tactical brilliance. However, he suffered defeats at Kolín (1757) and later faced the might of Russia's armies, which advanced deep into East Prussia.

Key Campaigns and Battles

- **Rossbach (November 1757)**: A small Prussian force decisively defeated a larger French-Imperial army in Saxony. The victory boosted Prussian morale and prestige across Europe, proving that Frederick's disciplined troops could outperform bigger coalition forces.
- **Leuthen (December 1757)**: Occurring just weeks after Rossbach, this battle saw Frederick outmaneuver a larger Austrian force in Silesia. The double-envelopment tactic and rapid flanking demonstrated Prussian excellence.
- **Zorndorf (1758)**: A bloody confrontation between Prussia and Russia, with extreme casualties on both sides. Although inconclusive, it showed that Prussia could hold its own against the Russians.
- **Kunersdorf (1759)**: In a devastating blow, a Russo-Austrian army inflicted one of Frederick's worst defeats. He reportedly despaired, fearing Prussia's collapse. But internal tensions within the coalition prevented them from capitalizing fully.

The "Miracle of the House of Brandenburg"

By 1760–1761, Prussia was on the brink of exhaustion. Berlin had been occupied briefly by Russian and Austrian troops. Frederick's treasury was nearly depleted, and manpower losses were severe. Yet in 1762, two major events changed the war's direction:

1. **Russia's Sudden Exit**: Tsarina Elizabeth died, and her successor, **Peter III**, admired Frederick II, withdrawing Russia from the conflict. Although Peter III was soon overthrown by Catherine the Great, Russia did not rejoin the war wholeheartedly.
2. **Financial Support from Britain**: Britain continued subsidizing Prussia's war effort, though tensions arose over costs.

This unexpected Russian about-face has often been called the "Miracle of the House of Brandenburg," saving Frederick from likely defeat. Prussia retained Silesia, and the final settlement recognized Frederick's state as a great power.

Section III: The Global Colonial Struggle – Britain vs. France

North America: The French and Indian War

In North America, the conflict was termed the **French and Indian War** (1754–1763), starting even before the Seven Years' War officially began in Europe. British colonies stretched along the Atlantic seaboard, while the French controlled Canada (New France) and claimed the vast Mississippi watershed. Skirmishes over the Ohio Valley sparked hostilities, as both sides allied with various Native American tribes.

- **Early French Successes**: Under commanders like Montcalm, the French initially triumphed at places like Fort Oswego and Fort William Henry. However, France struggled to supply its North American garrisons, as Britain's navy blockaded French ports.
- **British Resurgence**: In 1757, **William Pitt the Elder** became Britain's de facto war leader, injecting resources into colonial campaigns and focusing on sea power. Britain raised more colonial troops and leveraged its naval dominance to cut French supply lines.
- **Key Victories**:
    - **Fort Duquesne** fell and was renamed Fort Pitt (future Pittsburgh).
    - **Louisbourg (1758)**, a major fortress on Cape Breton Island, capitulated to a large British expedition, opening the Gulf of St. Lawrence.
    - **Battle of the Plains of Abraham (1759)** near Quebec City: General Wolfe's daring assault defeated Montcalm, leading to the fall of Quebec. Montreal followed in 1760, effectively ending French rule in Canada.

India: The Struggle of Trading Companies

Simultaneously, the British East India Company and the French Compagnie des Indes fought a proxy war, each supporting local Indian rulers and seeking commercial advantages.

- **Robert Clive** emerged as a key British figure, winning a significant victory at **Plassey (1757)** over the Nawab of Bengal, allied with the French. This success gave Britain control of Bengal's revenues, fueling further expansion.
- **Wandiwash (1760)** sealed French defeat in southern India, as British forces dismantled French strongholds. Although the French retained a few enclaves, they lost their broader Indian ambitions to the British.

The Caribbean and West Africa

In the Caribbean, the British captured French sugar islands such as Guadeloupe and Martinique at various points, though some were later returned by treaty. These islands were immensely valuable for sugar and rum production. Britain also seized the strategic French trading post of **Gorée** in West Africa.

Naval supremacy allowed Britain to blockade French trade routes, crippling French commerce and starving overseas garrisons. While France maintained a capable navy, it was outmatched by Britain's larger fleet and more robust financial system that could keep ships at sea longer.

Section IV: The End of the War and Peace Settlements

The Treaty of Paris (1763)

After years of fighting, France and Britain were both burdened by debt. Political changes in Britain led to negotiations for peace. In February 1763, the **Treaty of Paris** was signed between Britain, France, and Spain (which had entered the war in 1762 on France's side). The treaty's main provisions included:

- **North America**: France ceded Canada and all claims east of the Mississippi River to Britain, while Spain ceded Florida to Britain. In return, France gave Louisiana (the western Mississippi basin) to Spain.
- **India**: France lost most of its territorial footholds, retaining only small enclaves under strict commercial limitations.
- **Caribbean**: Britain returned some French sugar islands (like Guadeloupe and Martinique), recognizing their economic importance to France.
- **West Africa**: French coastal stations captured by Britain were returned, except for some minor rearrangements.

The Treaty of Hubertusburg (1763)

Separately, Prussia, Austria, and Saxony concluded the **Treaty of Hubertusburg (February 1763)**. This ended the continental war in Germany. Prussia retained Silesia, confirming Frederick II's greatest prize. The Holy Roman Empire's status quo was largely restored otherwise, marking no substantial territorial shift—yet it was a monumental diplomatic recognition of Prussia's new status as a European great power.

Section V: Consequences and Transformations

Britain's Ascendancy as a Global Power

The Seven Years' War cemented **Britain** as the world's foremost colonial empire. Holding Canada and dominance in India, Britain gained crucial trade routes and vast resources. However, managing and defending these territories required new policies and revenues, setting the stage for tensions with the American colonies—where British taxation measures would soon provoke the American Revolution (1775–1783).

Decline of French Colonial Ambitions

France's defeat was a severe blow. While France remained a major European land power, it lost most of its North American empire, part of its Indian presence, and faced crippling debt. French statesmen like the Duke of Choiseul recognized that the real cost was the strategic shift: Britain's naval superiority and colonial expansion had overshadowed France. The seeds of French financial crisis, partly fueled by war expenses, contributed to later instability that culminated in the French Revolution (1789).

Prussia's Rise in Germany

Frederick the Great emerged from the war with an enhanced reputation for military genius. Prussia's survival and retention of Silesia demonstrated it was no longer just another German state but a key power in central Europe. Austria's failure to reclaim Silesia confirmed its relative decline within the Holy Roman Empire, though Austria remained influential. The rivalry between Prussia and Austria would shape German affairs for decades, contributing to future conflicts over dominance in the German-speaking sphere.

Russia's First Foray into European Affairs

Russia's involvement marked its growing role in European power politics. Although Russia withdrew in 1762, the war showed how Russian armies could project force deep into central Europe. Under Catherine the Great (r. 1762–1796), Russia would expand further west and south, becoming a pivotal player in the continent's balance-of-power struggles.

Financial Strain and Political Repercussions

Nearly every participant emerged from the Seven Years' War burdened with massive debts. Britain, France, Austria, and others had to raise taxes or borrow extensively. These financial pressures sparked political unrest, for instance in Britain's North American colonies and in France's domestic economy. The war also illustrated the growing complexity of global conflict, where victories or losses in distant territories could decisively affect negotiations and alliances in Europe.

Section VI: Military and Diplomatic Innovations

Evolution of Warfare

The Seven Years' War continued the transition toward disciplined, linear musketry, bayonet charges, and coordinated artillery support. Prussia's efficient drilling, introduced by Frederick the Great, influenced European armies seeking to replicate his success. The concept of maneuver warfare advanced, with Frederick's "oblique order" tactics and strategic mobility providing repeated battlefield advantages.

Importance of Naval Power

The conflict underscored how **sea power** shaped outcomes. Britain's blockade of France, combined with control of the Atlantic, severely limited French reinforcement and supply to overseas colonies. Maritime supremacy allowed Britain to pick off French holdings one by one, from Canada to India. Naval might thus became a decisive factor in determining the war's global results.

Balance-of-Power Diplomacy Refined

The Diplomatic Revolution, where traditional enemies became allies, indicated that states now viewed alliances as fluid and based on pragmatic concerns rather than purely dynastic ties or historical enmities. The complex negotiations leading to the Treaties of Paris and Hubertusburg displayed the interplay between continental and colonial interests, reflecting a truly international perspective on warfare and peace settlements.

Section VII: Wider Global Context

Although often regarded as a European conflict, the Seven Years' War encompassed multiple continents. It tested the ability of states to wage war simultaneously across vast oceans. The East India Company's success in India spurred British expansion into the subcontinent, sowing seeds for the British Raj. In West Africa, the war shaped trade forts and local alliances, foreshadowing future colonial divisions. In the Caribbean, sugar colonies changed hands with each treaty, reflecting the commercial value of plantation economies.

Crucially, the war altered the dynamic in North America. With France removed as a major threat, British colonists felt less reliant on Britain's military protection. Soon, disputes over taxation and governance (to pay for the war's debt and manage new territories) led to colonial unrest. As a result, only a dozen years after the Treaty of Paris, Britain would face a revolutionary upheaval in its American colonies, culminating in the creation of the United States.

Section VIII: Aftermath and Long-Term Effects

British North America and the Road to Revolution

Britain's war debt prompted new taxes on American colonists—Stamp Act (1765), Townshend Acts (1767), etc.—leading to colonial protests. The removal of the French threat made the colonists less dependent on Britain for defense, fostering a sense of separate identity. These tensions accelerated toward the American Revolution, which erupted in 1775. Ironically, Britain's greatest victory over France set the stage for losing its most populous colonies.

French Financial Crisis and Discontent

For France, the war's debt burden intensified economic strains. The monarchy's attempts to reform taxation (for example under Turgot, then Necker) met aristocratic opposition. The memory of defeat also fueled a desire for revenge, leading France to support the American Revolution against Britain—a choice that further worsened French finances. By 1789, discontent over taxes, social inequalities, and the monarchy's failures contributed to the outbreak of the French Revolution.

Central Europe: Prussia's Prestige and Austria's Reforms

Frederick the Great's victory guaranteed that Prussia would be a dominant force in German affairs, rivaling the Habsburgs. Austria, meanwhile, recognized its limitations, leading Maria Theresa and her son Joseph II to implement Enlightenment-inspired reforms to strengthen the state internally. The rivalry between Hohenzollerns (Prussia) and Habsburgs (Austria) would persist well into the 19th century, shaping the path to German unification.

Worldwide Perspectives

The Seven Years' War set a precedent for conflicts fought on multiple continents, with alliances forged and broken over not just dynastic claims but also overseas trade and imperial competition. Later wars in the 18th and 19th centuries, such as the American Revolutionary War, Napoleonic Wars, and colonial struggles in Africa and Asia, would build on these patterns of global engagement.

Chapter 15: The Napoleonic Wars (Part 1) — From Revolutionary Roots to Imperial Dominance

Introduction

By the close of the 18th century, Europe had undergone wrenching changes. The French Revolution (1789) shattered the old order in France, toppling the monarchy and upending feudal structures. Across Europe, monarchies and aristocracies watched with alarm as revolutionary fervor spread. Amid the chaos, one military leader rose to the forefront: **Napoleon Bonaparte**, a Corsican-born artillery officer whose talent and ambition propelled him rapidly through the ranks of the French Revolutionary armies.

Although the **Revolutionary Wars** had already drawn much of Europe into conflict with the French Republic, the ascendancy of Napoleon would escalate these hostilities into what we now call the **Napoleonic Wars**. Spanning roughly 1799 to 1815, these wars redrew maps, toppled dynasties, and shaped nationalist sentiments. They also ushered in new approaches to warfare—emphasizing mass conscription, rapid maneuver, and the integration of politics and military strategy.

In this chapter, we trace Napoleon's early rise, from the last days of the French Revolutionary government (the Directory) through the establishment of the Consulate, culminating in his coronation as Emperor. We then explore the early coalitions that opposed him, the major battles that cemented his reputation, and the treaties that temporarily reshaped Europe between 1801 and 1807. This period set the stage for an even broader confrontation, one that would eventually see the tide turn against Napoleon—but not before he reached the zenith of imperial power.

Section I: From General to First Consul

The Coup of 18 Brumaire (1799)

By 1799, France had been at war with various European powers—Austria, Great Britain, Russia, the Ottoman Empire—since the onset of the Revolutionary Wars in 1792. The **Directory**, the five-man executive governing France, was increasingly unpopular due to corruption, economic woes, and military setbacks. Napoleon, already famous for successful campaigns in Italy (1796–1797) and for an audacious but ultimately difficult expedition to Egypt (1798–1799), took advantage of the discontent.

Returning from Egypt (where Britain's Admiral Nelson had disrupted French naval support by defeating the French fleet at the Battle of the Nile in 1798), Napoleon allied with key politicians and staged a coup on **18 Brumaire, Year VIII** of the Revolutionary calendar (9 November 1799). This coup dissolved the Directory and replaced it with the **Consulate**, effectively placing Napoleon as **First Consul**—the primary ruler of France.

Though the new government still claimed Revolutionary ideals, Napoleon concentrated power in his own hands. He introduced reforms to stabilize France: reorganizing the administration, improving tax collection, restoring the Church's position through the **Concordat of 1801** (though with strong state oversight), and enacting the **Napoleonic Code** (a unified legal system). These reforms garnered popular support, allowing him to mobilize France's resources for his military ventures.

The Second Coalition Unravels

At the time of Napoleon's coup, France was fighting the **Second Coalition** (primarily Austria, Britain, Russia, and others). Napoleon swiftly moved to secure peace on favorable terms. In 1800, he led an army across the Alps in a daring campaign, surprising Austrian forces in northern Italy. The decisive **Battle of Marengo (14 June 1800)** forced Austria to withdraw from much of Italy. Meanwhile, French armies under General Moreau pushed across the Rhine, defeating the Austrians at **Hohenlinden (3 December 1800)**.

Austria, exhausted and facing French armies deep in its territories, sued for peace. The **Treaty of Lunéville (1801)** confirmed French gains in Italy and along the Rhine. Russia had already withdrawn from the coalition, displeased with Britain's maritime policies and potential friction with Austria. Left largely isolated, Britain concluded an **Armistice of Amiens (1802)** with France, temporarily ending hostilities. For the first time in nearly a decade, Europe experienced a brief peace.

Section II: Emperor of the French and Renewed Conflict

The Path to Empire

Despite the Amiens peace, tensions between Britain and France simmered. Britain was suspicious of French colonial activities and did not fully dismantle its anti-French alliances or open trade. Napoleon, for his part, reorganized the French-dominated territories in Italy and Germany, placing loyal relatives or allies in positions of power. He also sold the **Louisiana Territory** to the United States in 1803, partly to deny Britain any chance of taking it if war resumed and partly to raise funds.

In 1804, having consolidated domestic control and increased his popularity, Napoleon crowned himself **Emperor of the French** at Notre-Dame Cathedral in Paris, in the presence of Pope Pius VII—but famously placing the crown on his own head. This act symbolized both the break from the old Bourbon monarchy and the assertion that Napoleon's power derived from his own deeds and the people's will (though heavily orchestrated).

Immediately, the Third Coalition against France began to form. Britain refused to recognize Napoleon's empire, resumed war in 1803, and soon allied with Austria and Russia. Sweden and other powers eventually joined as well. Napoleon prepared to invade Britain, amassing troops along the Channel coast near Boulogne. Yet the challenge lay in the Royal Navy's supremacy—crossing the Channel with a French fleet was a daunting prospect.

The Naval Dimension: Trafalgar (1805)

In 1805, a combined French-Spanish fleet attempted to break Britain's naval blockade, hoping to create a window for the invasion of England. However, Britain's Admiral Horatio Nelson intercepted them near Cape Trafalgar (off southwestern Spain). The **Battle of Trafalgar (21 October 1805)** proved a crushing British victory, though Nelson was killed in action. The battle confirmed British mastery of the seas; never again would Napoleon seriously attempt to invade the British Isles. Henceforth, Britain would remain safe from direct French attack, continuing as Napoleon's implacable maritime foe.

Section III: The Third Coalition and the Grande Armée's Triumphs

The Ulm Campaign (1805)

Even as he lost at sea, Napoleon sought quick victory on land. His **Grande Armée**, some 200,000 highly drilled troops, marched from the Channel coast to Germany with remarkable speed. In a swift maneuver, Napoleon surrounded an Austrian army under General Mack near **Ulm** (in Bavaria). By October 1805, the Austrians at Ulm surrendered en masse without a major pitched battle. This Ulm campaign showcased Napoleon's hallmark: rapid, decisive marches to encircle enemy forces.

The Battle of Austerlitz (1805)

Following Ulm, Napoleon advanced into Austrian territory. The Russians under Tsar Alexander I joined the Austrians, hoping to corner the French near Vienna. On **2 December 1805**, the Allies confronted Napoleon near the town of Austerlitz (modern-day Slavkov u Brna in the Czech Republic). This **Battle of Austerlitz**, also called the "Battle of the Three Emperors" (Napoleon, Alexander I, Emperor Francis II of Austria), is widely considered Napoleon's greatest victory.

Napoleon deliberately weakened his right flank, enticing the Allies to attack there. Then, with the Allied center exposed, the French delivered a devastating blow, splitting the Russian-Austrian line. The result was catastrophic for the Allies; entire columns were destroyed or forced to retreat chaotically. Casualty figures favored Napoleon decisively.

Austerlitz had enormous diplomatic repercussions. Austria soon sued for peace, signing the **Treaty of Pressburg (1805)**. The Holy Roman Empire effectively dissolved, replaced by the **Confederation of the Rhine**—a group of German states under French influence. Emperor Francis II relinquished the title of Holy Roman Emperor, becoming Francis I of Austria. Russia pulled back east, rethinking its role in the war. Napoleon's dominance on land now appeared unassailable.

Section IV: The Fourth Coalition (1806–1807)
The Fall of Prussia

Prussia, long neutral, grew alarmed at Napoleon's reordering of Germany. King Frederick William III decided to confront France, forming the **Fourth Coalition** with Britain, Russia, and others. Prussia mobilized its armies but lagged behind in adopting modern tactics. Napoleon marched swiftly across central Germany in October 1806, meeting the main Prussian forces at two simultaneous battles: **Jena** and **Auerstedt** (14 October 1806). The Prussians were soundly defeated, culminating in the occupation of Berlin by the French.

This debacle shocked Europe. Prussia, once respected for its military tradition (from Frederick the Great's era), collapsed in weeks. Napoleon confiscated key territories, abolished old structures, and pressed onward. He then introduced the **Continental System**, an economic blockade aimed at crippling Britain by prohibiting European trade with the British Isles. Through decrees such as the Berlin Decree (1806) and the Milan Decree (1807), Napoleon sought to starve British commerce. Yet enforcing this blockade across Europe required cooperation from many states—willing or otherwise—and sowed resentment.

The Polish Campaign and Eylau-Friedland

Russia continued fighting. By late 1806, Napoleon had moved into Polish territories (divided previously by Prussia and Russia in the Partitions of Poland). Poles welcomed the French, hoping Napoleon might restore Polish independence. The winter campaign of 1807 proved grueling. The **Battle of Eylau (7–8 February 1807)** was fought in a blizzard, degenerating into a brutal slog. Casualties were high on both sides, with no clear victor. Napoleon's aura of invincibility wavered slightly.

However, by summer Napoleon regained momentum. At the **Battle of Friedland (14 June 1807)**, he trapped a major Russian army against the Alle River, inflicting heavy losses. Tsar Alexander I, anxious to end the conflict, opened negotiations. The resulting **Treaties of Tilsit (July 1807)** brought peace (for the moment) between France and Russia; Alexander recognized Napoleon's continental gains and joined the Continental System, while Prussia was drastically reduced in size and forced to pay heavy indemnities.

Napoleon redrew the map again, creating the **Duchy of Warsaw** from Prussian-held Polish lands and awarding it to his ally, the King of Saxony. This arrangement further fueled Polish hopes for full independence under French patronage. Meanwhile, Russia agreed to aid France in pressuring Britain diplomatically—though it never fully complied.

Section V: Reshaping Europe Under French Hegemony

Confederation of the Rhine and Satellite Kingdoms

By 1807, much of mainland Europe lay under direct or indirect French control. Napoleon had formed the **Confederation of the Rhine**, effectively making southwestern and western Germany a French satellite. He installed relatives on various thrones:

- **Joseph Bonaparte** became King of Naples (then, later, King of Spain).
- **Louis Bonaparte** ruled the Kingdom of Holland.
- **Jerome Bonaparte** served as King of Westphalia (a new realm carved out of central Germany).

In Italy, Napoleon was King of Italy (in addition to Emperor of the French), while his stepson, **Eugène de Beauharnais**, was Viceroy. The Papal States bristled under French dominance, leading to tensions with Pope Pius VII. Switzerland, reorganized as the Helvetic Confederation, also fell under French sway.

The Continental System in Practice

Despite these sweeping changes, the Continental System proved difficult to enforce. Britain still commanded the seas, enabling smuggling and alternative trade routes. Countries like Portugal, dependent on British commerce, refused to comply. Even Napoleon's allies found the blockade detrimental to their own economies. Tensions simmered across the continent, with some regions chafing under French-imposed tariffs and restrictions.

Moreover, Britain retaliated with **Orders in Council**, mandating that neutral ships must pass through British ports before trading with Europe, effectively blockading the continent. This standoff caused disruptions to global commerce, hurting neutral nations like the United States and fueling resentment that eventually contributed to the War of 1812 (though that is a separate conflict).

Section VI: Military Innovations and the Grande Armée

Organization and Tactics

Napoleon's success hinged on the formidable **Grande Armée**, a force that at times numbered over half a million men (though rarely all in the same theater). Napoleon's approach to warfare involved:

1. **Corps System**: The army was divided into self-contained corps, each with its own infantry, cavalry, and artillery. Marshals commanded these corps, enabling rapid, flexible maneuvers.
2. **Concentration in Time and Space**: Napoleon massed his corps quickly at critical points, overwhelming enemies before they could combine forces.
3. **Focus on the Offensive**: Aggressive maneuvering forced the enemy to react, often leading to encirclement or forced retreats.

Officers were promoted based on merit—at least more so than in many older monarchies—earning Napoleon loyalty and a steady supply of able subordinates. Soldiers were conscripted through the **levée en masse** (from the Revolutionary period) and subsequent annual drafts. Patriotism, the lure of glory, and battlefield success kept morale high, although casualties were frequently appalling.

Marshals and Key Commanders

Napoleon's marshals—Ney, Lannes, Soult, Davout, Murat, and others—gained fame for their battlefield prowess. Marshal Davout, for instance, performed brilliantly at Auerstedt, defeating a larger Prussian force. Marshal Lannes was known for unwavering bravery, but also for strategic acumen. Marshal Murat led cavalry charges with flamboyant style. Each marshal had distinct strengths, and Napoleon allocated tasks accordingly, relying on their ability to carry out independent missions within his overarching strategy.

Section VII: Assessing the Empire's Apex (1807)

By mid-1807, Napoleon's empire sprawled from the Atlantic coast of Portugal (though not yet conquered) to the borders of Russia, from the Baltic Sea to southern Italy. Only Britain stood openly defiant, protected by the Royal Navy. Austria, though humiliated, watched for a chance to strike back; Russia, newly allied, harbored doubts about the French partnership. Prussia was prostrate but simmering with discontent. Many Germans resented French dominance; Spanish patriots bristled under Bourbon reorganization; and across Europe, intellectuals debated whether Napoleon brought "enlightenment" or merely a new brand of tyranny.

In the next chapter, we will see how this apex began to unravel. From the invasion of the Iberian Peninsula to the ill-fated campaign in Russia, Napoleon's overreach and the resilience of his adversaries would transform Europe yet again. But for now, in 1807, the Napoleonic Empire seemed the pinnacle of modern warfare and statecraft, a testament to one man's ambition—hailed by admirers, feared by rivals, and endured by those forced under French hegemony.

Chapter 16: The Napoleonic Wars (Part 2) — From Iberian Quagmire to the Fall of the Empire

Introduction

Having reached the year 1807, Napoleon Bonaparte's empire appeared at its zenith. France and its satellite states ringed Europe, from the shores of the Baltic Sea to the Italian peninsula. Russia stood as a nominal ally after the Treaties of Tilsit, and Prussia was reduced to a vassal-like condition. Yet under this impressive façade, tensions festered. The Continental System disrupted commerce, fueling resentment among allies and neutrals alike. Traditional powers like Austria yearned for revenge, and Russia's Tsar Alexander I harbored misgivings about the French alliance. Perhaps most significant, Napoleon's own ambitions led him into new ventures that overextended his resources.

In this second part of our exploration of the Napoleonic Wars, we follow Napoleon's empire from its pinnacle into the protracted Peninsular War, the catastrophic Russian invasion, the subsequent Coalition victories, and the Emperor's ultimate defeat at Waterloo in 1815. We will see how local insurrections, shifting alliances, and the resilience of states forced to the brink of collapse eventually combined to topple Europe's most formidable conqueror of the age.

Section I: The Peninsular War (1808–1814)

The Portuguese Gateway

Napoleon's Continental System demanded that all ports be closed to British trade. **Portugal**, historically allied with Britain, refused to comply fully. In late 1807, Napoleon coerced Spain's weak Bourbon government into permitting French troops to cross Spanish territory and occupy Portugal. The Portuguese royal family fled to Brazil, but the French presence in the Iberian Peninsula quickly expanded far beyond the initial plan.

Realizing the strategic importance of controlling Spain itself, Napoleon entangled French forces in Spanish politics. He maneuvered the Spanish royal family—King Charles IV and his son Ferdinand VII—into abdicating in 1808, placing his brother **Joseph Bonaparte** on the Spanish throne. This blatant takeover outraged Spaniards across social classes, sparking a fierce patriotic revolt. The stage was set for a grueling conflict that historians call the **Peninsular War**.

Uprisings and Guerrilla Warfare

Spain erupted in revolt in May 1808. Local juntas (councils) formed to resist French authority, and savage street fighting broke out in cities like Madrid. Napoleon dispatched large numbers of troops to suppress the rebellion, expecting a quick victory. Although the French initially overwhelmed Spanish regular forces, they soon faced a new challenge: **guerrilla warfare**.

Spanish partisans, often supported by local populations, ambushed French detachments, cut supply lines, and exacted a heavy toll in repeated raids. The word "guerrilla" (little war) entered the lexicon to describe these small-scale, hit-and-run tactics. The French found themselves unable to pacify the countryside, even though they controlled major cities. This made the Peninsular War a constant drain on French manpower and resources.

British Intervention: Sir Arthur Wellesley

The British saw an opportunity to strike Napoleon on the continent, while also supporting their Portuguese allies. **Sir Arthur Wellesley** (later the Duke of Wellington) led a small expeditionary force that landed in Portugal in August 1808. In battles like **Roliça** and **Vimeiro**, the British defeated French troops under General Junot, forcing an agreement (the Convention of Cintra) that compelled French withdrawal from Portugal.

Napoleon took personal command that autumn, leading an army of over 200,000 into Spain. He achieved a series of victories, retook Madrid, and forced the British to retreat. But the Emperor soon withdrew to address other concerns in Central Europe, leaving marshals in charge. This partial success proved illusory; British forces returned, and Spanish guerrillas persisted.

By 1810–1811, Marshall Masséna tried to drive the British from Portugal but failed, culminating in the lines of Torres Vedras, formidable defensive works near

Lisbon built under Wellington's direction. The French were forced to retreat, losing tens of thousands in the process. Over the next years, Wellington's Anglo-Portuguese army gradually pushed the French out of Portugal and into Spain, while Spanish guerrillas tied down entire French divisions.

A War of Attrition

The Peninsular War became a quagmire for Napoleon. Spanish nationalism, British subsidies, local knowledge of terrain, and the constant harassment by partisans turned the Iberian Peninsula into a "Spanish Ulcer"—a bleeding wound draining French resources. Historians estimate Napoleon cycled over 300,000 troops through Spain during the war. Many never returned. This protracted conflict not only shattered the myth of French invincibility but also emboldened other states to consider renewed resistance.

Section II: The War of the Fifth Coalition and Austrian Resurgence (1809)

Austrian Gamble

While the French were bogged down in Iberia, Austria seized the moment to rebuild its army under the guidance of reformers like Archduke Charles and Johann von Hiller. In early 1809, it launched an offensive in Bavaria, hoping to rekindle a German uprising against Napoleon. The **Fifth Coalition** included Britain (financing Austria and continuing the struggle in Iberia) and various minor German states that quietly aided Austrian intelligence or supplies.

Napoleon, reacting swiftly, hurried from Paris and directed the Grande Armée in a series of lightning moves. In April and May 1809, French forces clashed with the Austrians in Bavaria, culminating in the battles of **Eckmühl** and **Ratisbon**. The French overcame initial setbacks, forcing the Austrians to retreat.

Aspern-Essling and Wagram

Crossing the Danube near Vienna, Napoleon encountered the main Austrian army. The **Battle of Aspern-Essling (21–22 May 1809)** was a rare check on Napoleon's record. The Austrians, led by Archduke Charles, repulsed repeated French attacks. Marshal Lannes was mortally wounded. Napoleon's forces withdrew to an island in the Danube. Despite losing the battle, the Emperor soon resumed the offensive, reorganizing his supply lines.

A few weeks later, Napoleon forced another crossing, leading to the **Battle of Wagram (5–6 July 1809)**. This brutal confrontation saw immense artillery exchanges and massed attacks. Eventually, superior French coordination and heavier concentration of fire broke the Austrian lines. Archduke Charles retreated, prompting Austria to negotiate once again.

The Treaty of Schönbrunn (1809)

Despite its gallant effort, Austria had to sign another punitive treaty. The **Treaty of Schönbrunn** stripped Austrian territories, gave some lands to Bavaria and Saxony, and forced marriage ties: Napoleon divorced his first wife, Josephine, and married the Austrian Archduchess **Marie Louise** in 1810, hoping to legitimize his dynasty and cement an alliance. Although temporarily subdued, Austria remained resentful and awaited a future alliance with other powers—especially if Napoleon's fortunes waned.

Section III: The Russian Campaign (1812)

Growing Tensions with Tsar Alexander I

After Tilsit (1807), France and Russia had an uneasy partnership. Alexander I initially cooperated with the Continental System but grew frustrated by its economic damage. Meanwhile, Napoleon's expansions in Poland (the Duchy of Warsaw) alarmed Russia, which saw itself as Poland's rightful overlord. Disagreements over control in the Balkans, the Eastern Mediterranean, and over marriage alliances (Alexander refused to give his sister in marriage to Napoleon) further strained relations.

Napoleon, determined to enforce the Continental System, suspected Russia was secretly trading with Britain. By 1811, both sides mobilized. In June 1812, Napoleon led an army of over 600,000 soldiers—drawn from across his empire—into Russia. The **Grand Army** included Poles, Germans, Italians, Dutch, Swiss, and others. The campaign's stated goal: force Alexander to comply with the blockade. Unofficially, Napoleon aimed to humble Russia once and for all, securing total dominance on the continent.

The March to Moscow

The Russians, under Generals Barclay de Tolly and Bagration, adopted a scorched-earth policy: retreating while destroying crops and supplies, denying the French sustenance. A few engagements, like **Smolensk (August 1812)**, offered no decisive clash. The French advanced deep into Russia, coping with extreme heat, dust, and supply breakdowns.

Finally, the Russians made a stand at **Borodino (7 September 1812)**, about 100 kilometers west of Moscow. This battle was a brutal slog, with casualties reaching tens of thousands on each side. Although the French forced a Russian withdrawal, it was a costly "victory"—there was no decisive annihilation of the Russian army. Napoleon pressed on to Moscow, hoping to force Alexander to negotiate.

On **14 September 1812**, the Grande Armée entered Moscow. To their shock, the city was largely abandoned by civilians, and soon fires broke out in multiple quarters. Whether ordered by the governor, by some Russian patriots, or by chance, the burning of Moscow denied the French a winter haven. Napoleon waited in vain for a peace offer that never came. As weeks passed, supplies ran low, discipline frayed, and the Russian winter loomed.

The Retreat from Moscow

By mid-October, with no negotiations, Napoleon ordered a retreat. The journey back proved catastrophic. Freezing temperatures, lack of food, constant harassment by Russian light cavalry, and the lingering threat of renewed Russian offensives decimated the once-mighty Grande Armée. Thousands died daily from hunger, cold, or disease. The crossing of the **Berezina River** in November was especially harrowing, as partial pontoon bridges struggled to hold the mass of retreating troops. Only a fraction of the original force returned to friendly soil, many in rags or severely wounded.

The Russian campaign shattered Napoleon's aura of invincibility. States across Europe sensed the coming collapse of French hegemony. Prussia, forcibly allied to France after Jena, now prepared to switch sides. Austria also inched closer to renewed war. Britain saw an opening to redouble efforts in Spain. The stage was set for a massive confrontation.

Section IV: The War of the Sixth Coalition (1813–1814)

Rebellion in Germany

In early 1813, Napoleon attempted to rebuild his army. Despite the catastrophic losses in Russia, he conscripted fresh levies from France and allied states. Meanwhile, the **Sixth Coalition** formed, including Russia, Prussia, Britain, Sweden (under Crown Prince Bernadotte, ironically a former French marshal), and eventually Austria. German nationalists, long resentful of French occupation, viewed this as a war of liberation.

Napoleon achieved some initial successes at **Lützen** and **Bautzen** (May 1813) against Russian and Prussian forces, but these victories were less decisive than in previous wars. The French recruits lacked the experience of earlier Grande Armée veterans. A summer armistice provided a brief pause, during which Austria attempted mediation. When negotiations failed, Austria joined the Allies.

The Battle of Leipzig (1813)

The campaign resumed in August 1813. Napoleon maneuvered in Saxony, hoping to defeat coalition armies piecemeal. However, at the **Battle of Leipzig (16–19 October 1813)**—often called the "Battle of the Nations"—the combined forces of Austria, Prussia, Russia, and Sweden converged on Napoleon. Fighting raged for days around the city's outskirts. Outnumbered and short on cavalry, Napoleon could not hold off the Allies. On the final day, a critical bridge was blown prematurely, trapping part of the French rearguard. The French retreated west, leaving 80,000 casualties (French and Allied) in the largest European battle before World War I.

Leipzig marked the decisive break of French control in Germany. The Confederation of the Rhine collapsed as its member states switched sides. Napoleon retreated toward France with a battered army, facing a resurgent coalition determined to end his dominance.

The Invasion of France (1814)

Allied armies crossed the Rhine in late 1813 and early 1814. Napoleon, demonstrating his old brilliance, fought a "Campaign of France," achieving remarkable local victories in battles like Champaubert and Montmirail. Yet the Allies pressed relentlessly. By March, they entered Paris. Political forces in the capital turned against Napoleon. Marshals and high officials urged him to abdicate, believing continued resistance hopeless.

On **6 April 1814**, Napoleon abdicated unconditionally. The Allies restored the Bourbon monarchy under **Louis XVIII** (brother of the executed Louis XVI). Napoleon was exiled to the island of **Elba**, off the Tuscan coast.

The Hundred Days and the Seventh Coalition (1815)

Despite his exile to Elba, Napoleon's story was not yet over. Elba, a small island off the coast of Tuscany, allowed Napoleon a modest court and a tiny personal guard, yet his ambition still burned. In France, the restored Bourbon monarchy under **Louis XVIII** struggled to garner popular support. Memories of the Revolution remained fresh, and many war veterans, officers, and commoners alike felt nostalgia for the glory days of the Empire. Economic troubles, resentment over lost territories, and fears that old privileges would fully return under Bourbon rule further eroded Louis XVIII's position.

Napoleon's Return from Elba

Sensing this discontent, Napoleon made a bold move. On **26 February 1815**, he slipped away from Elba with a small force, landing in southern France near Golfe-Juan on 1 March. As he marched north, soldiers sent to arrest him instead rallied to his side, recalling their former Emperor's leadership. Famously, Napoleon confronted one royalist battalion, opened his coat, and declared: "If any of you would shoot your Emperor, do it now." Instead, the troops cheered for him.

This dramatic march toward Paris became known as the **Route Napoléon**. Marshal Ney, who initially pledged to capture Napoleon, soon defected with his men. Louis XVIII fled the capital on 19 March, and the very next day Napoleon re-entered Paris, reestablishing himself in power without a single shot fired against him. This sudden reclamation of authority is called the **Hundred Days**—a brief but intense period from March to June 1815 during which Napoleon attempted to rebuild his empire and consolidate the loyalty of France once again.

Formation of the Seventh Coalition

Europe's rulers reacted with alarm. Having exiled Napoleon once, they were determined not to let him destabilize the continent again. Britain, Austria,

Russia, and Prussia—joined by other states—formed a new alliance, the **Seventh Coalition**, pledging to field vast armies to overthrow Napoleon once and for all. Meanwhile, inside France, Napoleon tried to reassure moderates by adopting a somewhat more constitutional stance, granting a revised Charter in hopes of winning broader support. But time was short. Vast Coalition forces were already mobilizing.

Napoleon believed his best chance lay in striking before the Coalition armies could fully unite. He especially focused on the Anglo-Dutch forces under **Arthur Wellesley, Duke of Wellington**, positioned in the Belgian Low Countries, and the Prussian army under **Gebhard Leberecht von Blücher**, stationed nearby. If he could defeat these armies in detail, perhaps he might force a negotiated settlement, or so he hoped.

The Waterloo Campaign (June 1815)

Strategic Overview

Napoleon gathered an army of around 120,000 men, referred to as the **Armée du Nord**, and crossed the frontier into modern-day Belgium in mid-June 1815. His plan involved a rapid advance to split the Anglo-Dutch and Prussian armies, defeating each separately. Wellington and Blücher had approximately 210,000 troops combined, but they were spread out, still maneuvering to concentrate. Should Napoleon catch them unprepared, he could replicate his classic strategy of swift strikes for partial victories.

The initial engagements occurred on 15–16 June at **Quatre Bras** (where Wellington's forces fought Marshal Ney) and **Ligny** (where Napoleon personally defeated Blücher's Prussians). At Ligny, the Prussians were forced to retreat, suffering heavy casualties. However, crucially, they were not destroyed, nor did they flee eastward as Napoleon expected. Instead, Blücher marched north to maintain contact with Wellington, coordinating future action. This decision would prove decisive.

The Battle of Waterloo (18 June 1815)

On **18 June 1815**, Napoleon confronted Wellington's Anglo-Dutch army near the village of **Waterloo**, south of Brussels. Wellington positioned his forces along a ridge, using farmhouses and terrain folds for cover. The ground, soaked by recent rain, delayed Napoleon's attack until midday, giving the Prussians extra time to march in support of Wellington.

1. **Initial Assaults**: Marshal Ney directed French infantry columns against the Allied left at the farmhouse of **Hougoumont**, intending it as a diversion. Yet Hougoumont became a bitter, protracted fight, devouring French units that might have been used elsewhere. In the center, repeated French attacks struggled against Allied infantry deployed behind the ridge.
2. **D'Erlon's Attack and the Allied Squares**: Later, General d'Erlon led a massive French assault on Wellington's center-right. Allied units formed defensive squares to repel French cavalry. Despite severe pressure, the Anglo-Dutch line held. Ney, believing the Allies were collapsing, launched cavalry charges prematurely—only to see them repulsed by solid infantry squares and well-placed artillery.
3. **Arrival of the Prussians**: By late afternoon, Blücher's Prussian vanguard began arriving at **Plancenoit**, on Napoleon's right flank. This development forced Napoleon to divert reserves, including part of the elite Imperial Guard, to contain the Prussians. As the Prussian force increased, the French right began to buckle.
4. **Imperial Guard's Final Charge**: Near evening, Napoleon ordered his Imperial Guard—his most loyal, battle-hardened troops—to assault Wellington's center in a final bid for victory. Under heavy fire, the Guard faltered. Allied troops, rising from concealed positions, delivered devastating volleys. The Guard retreated in disorder, signaling the collapse of French morale. Wellington then advanced, coordinating with the steadily growing Prussian presence.
5. **Complete French Rout**: Once the Guard fell back, the French army disintegrated. Many soldiers fled in panic. Only a fraction escaped the battlefield. Napoleon, recognizing defeat, withdrew with the remnants of the Armée du Nord.

Waterloo sealed Napoleon's fate. His once-legendary luck and skill could not overcome the combined tenacity of Wellington, Blücher, and the resolute Allied forces. The battle was catastrophic for the French: some 25,000 casualties and tens of thousands captured or missing. The Allies also suffered heavily but had achieved final victory.

Section V: Napoleon's Final Downfall and Exile

Abdication and the Second Bourbon Restoration

News of Waterloo's result quickly reached Paris, sparking turmoil. Leading officials and marshals recognized that any further resistance was impossible. On **22 June 1815**, Napoleon abdicated in favor of his young son, Napoleon II—though this claim was never recognized by the Allies. Louis XVIII returned to Paris, beginning the **Second Restoration** of the Bourbon monarchy. Determined to avoid another Elba fiasco, the Allies insisted that Napoleon must be exiled far away from Europe.

The Voyage to Saint Helena

Attempting to escape to the United States, Napoleon discovered the ports closely monitored by the British Royal Navy. On **15 July 1815**, he surrendered himself aboard the British warship HMS Bellerophon, hoping for more lenient treatment. However, Britain, with Allied consent, decided to send him to **Saint Helena**, a remote island in the South Atlantic. In October 1815, Napoleon arrived there, effectively cut off from any power base or possibility of return. A handful of loyal companions accompanied him.

On Saint Helena, Napoleon lived under constant British supervision. He spent his final years dictating memoirs, pondering his campaigns, and engaging in conversations with his small entourage. He died on **5 May 1821**, possibly from stomach cancer (though other theories have circulated). With his passing, the Napoleonic epoch truly ended—though legends, myths, and debates about his reign endured.

Section VI: The Congress of Vienna and the Reshaping of Europe

During Napoleon's final downfall, the Allies convened the **Congress of Vienna** (1814–1815) to restore stability to Europe and prevent any single power from dominating again. Key figures included Austria's Prince Metternich, Britain's Lord Castlereagh, Russia's Tsar Alexander I, Prussia's Hardenberg, and France's Talleyrand. While Napoleon temporarily escaped Elba (thus interrupting the congress), the final settlement was concluded after Waterloo.

Main Aims and Agreements

1. **Legitimacy**: The old dynasties were mostly restored to their thrones (the Bourbons in France, Spain, Naples, etc.).
2. **Balance of Power**: Borders were redrawn to create states strong enough to check one another. Prussia gained territory in the Rhineland, Austria reasserted control over northern Italy, and a loose German Confederation replaced the Napoleonic-era Confederation of the Rhine.
3. **Containment of France**: The Allies ringed France with stronger neighbors. The Kingdom of the Netherlands combined the old Dutch Republic and Austrian Netherlands, forming a buffer in the north. Piedmont-Sardinia was strengthened in the south-east.
4. **No Excessive Punishment for France**: Talleyrand's diplomatic skill and the Allies' fear of creating long-term resentment meant France retained its 1792 borders and avoided ruinous reparations (beyond a moderate indemnity and the stationing of occupation troops).

The **Concert of Europe**—an informal system of consultation among the great powers—emerged, aiming to preserve the new status quo and stave off major continental wars. While tensions and conflicts still arose, the Napoleonic Wars' devastation led these powers to cooperate in suppressing revolutionary movements and maintaining general peace for several decades.

Section VII: Impact and Legacy of the Napoleonic Wars

Death Toll and Societal Changes

The Napoleonic Wars inflicted immense suffering across Europe. Estimates vary, but several million soldiers and civilians died between 1792 and 1815. Entire regions were ravaged repeatedly by armies foraging and fighting. Political upheavals—monarchies falling, republics rising, then empires forming—shaped the 19th century. Many states, forced to modernize their armies and bureaucracies in response to France, continued these reforms afterwards.

At the same time, the wars spread certain Revolutionary ideals, such as the abolition of feudal privileges, the Napoleonic Code's legal standards, and broader concepts of nationalism. Peoples under French occupation sometimes adopted or resisted French-imposed changes, contributing to the spread of nationalist consciousness. For instance, in Germany and Italy, the rearrangement of states awakened aspirations for unification. In Spain and Latin America, the Napoleonic invasion triggered independence movements in Spanish colonies.

Nationalism and the Military

Napoleon's mass conscription model and the emphasis on patriotic fervor laid groundwork for later 19th-century national armies. The success of large, citizen-based forces (instead of small professional armies) demonstrated the power of mobilizing entire populations. However, the Napoleonic approach also showed the dangers of militarizing society, as repeated wars consumed manpower and resources, leaving Europe exhausted by 1815.

The Diplomatic Model

The coalitions against Napoleon showcased the evolution of multi-state alliances. Nations with divergent interests united under a common goal: defeating France's hegemonic ambitions. After 1815, the great powers sought to maintain equilibrium through the **Concert of Europe**—a pattern of congresses and treaties that managed tensions for much of the 19th century. Though not always successful, it represented an early form of collective security.

Section VIII: The Transformation of Warfare

The Napoleonic era revolutionized warfare. Key changes included:

1. **Corps Organization**: As noted, dividing armies into self-contained corps gave flexibility and speed, enabling rapid concentration at critical points.
2. **Logistics and Foraging**: Napoleon's armies often lived off the land, allowing them to move swiftly without waiting for large supply convoys. However, this strategy proved perilous in areas with scorched earth tactics (as in Russia).
3. **Combined Arms Tactics**: French doctrine integrated artillery, cavalry, and infantry more cohesively than many adversaries at the start. Over time, states like Austria and Prussia adapted, leveling the playing field.
4. **Conscription and Patriotism**: The levée en masse begun in the Revolution gave France a massive pool of manpower. Eventually, other nations like Prussia introduced similar systems, reflecting a shift toward national armies.

The Napoleonic Wars thus bridged earlier 18th-century limited conflict (with smaller professional armies) and the total, mass warfare more characteristic of later eras.

Section IX: The Global Dimension

While primarily centered in Europe, the Napoleonic Wars had global ramifications. Britain's naval supremacy extended the conflict to overseas colonies, with battles or occupations in the Caribbean, Africa, and Asia. The War of 1812 in North America, partly influenced by Britain's maritime blockade and tensions with the United States, further underscored the period's worldwide impact.

Moreover, the Haitian Revolution (1791–1804), which led to Haiti's independence, was tied to the broader crisis of the French Revolution. Napoleon tried (and failed) to reconquer Saint-Domingue, leading to the Louisiana Purchase (1803) that reshaped North America's map. Spanish colonies in the Americas seized the moment of Spain's turmoil to launch independence movements—events that would transform the Western Hemisphere in the early 19th century.

Section X: Conclusion — The End of an Era

By the time Napoleon Bonaparte died in exile on Saint Helena in 1821, Europe had already embarked on a new chapter. The Bourbon Restoration in France never fully recaptured the old regime's character, and a generation of French citizens had grown up under Revolutionary and Imperial rule. Across the continent, new boundaries drawn at Vienna, combined with the memory of the Napoleonic Wars, shaped a century of relative peace among great powers—punctuated by smaller-scale conflicts, revolutions, and unification movements.

The Napoleonic Wars, spanning from 1799 to 1815 in their strict sense (or even 1792 if including the Revolutionary Wars), remain some of the most studied in history. They brought forth towering figures—Napoleon himself, Wellington, Nelson, Kutuzov, Blücher—and epic battles—Austerlitz, Jena, Eylau, Borodino, Waterloo. They also unleashed ideological forces that would mold modern Europe: nationalism, liberal reform, and the concept of large-scale conscript armies. For better or worse, the Napoleonic era forged the path for the 19th century, setting frameworks for both states' development and future conflicts.

In reflecting on these two chapters, we see how Napoleon rose from a modest Corsican officer to become Emperor of the French, dominating the European continent like few before him. Yet the same qualities that fueled his success—unrelenting ambition, strategic audacity—ultimately drove him into ruinous campaigns, particularly in Spain and Russia. The coalition wars hammered home the lesson that no single power could sustain total hegemony if confronted by united adversaries. When the final reckoning came at Waterloo, it was a coalition effort that ensured Napoleon's star had set.

Hence, the Napoleonic Wars concluded a revolutionary epoch in European history, ushering in a new balance of power. The old monarchies returned, but seeds of change—national self-determination, constitutionalism, mass participation in warfare—would continue growing, eventually reshaping politics, society, and warfare over the following decades. Napoleon's legacy, both admired and reviled, is woven into the very fabric of modern Europe and remains a defining reference point in the study of military genius, statecraft, and the colossal costs of seemingly perpetual war.

Chapter 17: Conflicts in the 19th Century — From the Greek War of Independence to the Franco-Prussian War

Introduction

When Napoleon Bonaparte fell in 1815, Europe's political map had been radically altered, and statesmen at the **Congress of Vienna** hoped to restore stability by reasserting traditional monarchies and borders. Yet beneath this conservative veneer, forces unleashed during the Revolutionary and Napoleonic period—nationalism, liberal reform, and the desire for self-determination—continued to simmer. Over the next decades, various regions experienced wars for independence, unity, or autonomy, alongside efforts by conservative powers to suppress such movements.

In this chapter, we will explore some of the major conflicts that rocked Europe from the end of the Napoleonic era until the late 19th century. We begin with the **Greek War of Independence**, a dramatic struggle against Ottoman rule that attracted romantic support from across the continent. We will then examine the 1848 revolutions and their consequences, the **Crimean War** that disrupted the balance set by the Congress of Vienna, and finally the wars that reshaped central Europe—particularly Italy's unification struggles and the **Franco-Prussian War**, which sealed the fate of the Second French Empire and led to the rise of a new, unified Germany. Through these conflicts, the 19th century laid the groundwork for modern nation-states, rewriting borders and identities that had seemed fixed at the close of the Napoleonic Wars.

Section I: The Greek War of Independence (1821–1832)

Ottoman Background and Growing Discontent

For centuries, the Greek-speaking populations in southeastern Europe and the Aegean islands lived under the control of the **Ottoman Empire**. While some Greeks prospered as merchants or functionaries within the empire, many resented Ottoman authority, heavy taxation, and the second-class status of Christian communities under Muslim rule. Inspired by the ideals of the Enlightenment, the French Revolution, and earlier Balkan uprisings (such as the Serbian revolt against Ottoman rule), Greek patriots began organizing secret societies. Among these was the **Filiki Eteria** (Society of Friends), founded in 1814 with the aim of igniting a widespread rebellion.

Outbreak of Revolt

In March 1821, revolutionaries launched uprisings in multiple regions: the Peloponnese, central Greece, and parts of what is now southern Romania (Moldavia and Wallachia). While the attempt in the Danubian principalities quickly faltered, the revolt in the Peloponnese (the Morea) gained momentum. Greek insurgents captured towns and massacred some Ottoman garrisons, prompting brutal reprisals from the Ottoman authorities. The fighting was marked by atrocities on both sides, stoking the fires of a war viewed in Europe as a Christian struggle against "Turkish tyranny."

International Attention and Romantic Philhellenism

Despite initial reluctance by major European powers to support revolutionary movements (since these powers were committed to the "legitimacy" principle of the **Concert of Europe**), the Greek cause gained sympathy among intellectuals, artists, and liberal politicians. Romantic writers like **Lord Byron** championed Greek independence, seeing Greece as the cradle of Western civilization. Volunteers from Germany, Britain, and France traveled to fight alongside Greek insurgents, forming a wave of **Philhellenism** that pressured governments to reconsider their positions.

Moreover, Russia had long viewed itself as a protector of Orthodox Christians in the Ottoman Empire. Though wary of revolutionary contagion, Tsar Alexander I and later Tsar Nicholas I recognized an opportunity to exert influence. Britain and France, for their part, balanced their desire to contain Russia with the popular appeal of aiding the Greeks.

Turning Points: Navarino and International Intervention

Early in the war, Greek forces managed to establish a provisional government, but internal rivalries hindered unity. The Ottomans, assisted by their Egyptian vassal **Mehmet Ali** (who sent a modernized Egyptian fleet and troops), regained ground, recapturing key Greek strongholds. By the mid-1820s, the Greek cause teetered on the brink of collapse.

However, a shift occurred when Britain, France, and Russia decided—largely under public pressure and some strategic calculations—to intervene diplomatically. In 1827, their combined fleets encountered the Ottoman-Egyptian navy at the **Battle of Navarino** off the Peloponnese. The Allied fleets sank most of the Ottoman-Egyptian ships, effectively crippling Ottoman sea power in the region. This victory, while portrayed by Allied governments as an "accidental" engagement, was decisive in saving the Greeks from defeat.

Final Phases and Independence

After Navarino, Russia declared war on the Ottoman Empire (the Russo-Turkish War of 1828–1829), advancing through the Balkans and the Caucasus. Under combined military and diplomatic pressure, the Sublime Porte (Ottoman government) conceded Greek autonomy in negotiations. By 1832, the **Treaty of Constantinople** officially recognized Greece as an independent kingdom, with a Bavarian prince, **Otto**, chosen as its monarch.

The Greek War of Independence thus became a milestone in the 19th-century movement toward national self-determination. It also marked a breach in the conservative unity of Europe's great powers, showing that public opinion and romantic ideals could push governments to support a revolutionary cause—at least when it aligned with strategic interests.

Section II: The Revolutions of 1848 and Their Consequences

Widespread Discontent

Across Europe, the 1830s and 1840s witnessed growing unrest. The Industrial Revolution had transformed economies in Britain, Belgium, and parts of Germany, leading to urbanization and social pressures. Agricultural crises, notably the **Irish Potato Famine** (1845–1849), added severe hardship. Middle-class liberals demanded constitutional reforms, freedom of the press, and expanded suffrage, while working classes—often unemployed or underpaid—agitated for better conditions. Nationalist movements flourished in multi-ethnic states like the Austrian Empire, where Hungarians, Czechs, and Italians sought greater autonomy.

The Spark in France

In February 1848, protests in Paris against the repressive policies of King Louis Philippe escalated into an uprising. The monarch abdicated, and revolutionaries proclaimed the **Second Republic** in France. This event set off a chain reaction across Europe—commonly known as the **Revolutions of 1848** or the "Springtime of the Peoples."

- **German States**: In March 1848, demonstrations in Berlin forced King Frederick William IV of Prussia to make liberal concessions. Representatives from various German states convened the **Frankfurt Parliament**, aiming to unite Germany under a constitution. However, internal disputes between "Greater Germany" (including Austria) and "Lesser Germany" (excluding Austria) complicated progress.
- **Austrian Empire**: In Vienna, student protests and worker unrest toppled Prince Metternich's conservative regime. Hungary, under Lajos Kossuth, declared autonomy, while Italians in Lombardy-Venetia revolted against Austrian rule.
- **Italian States**: Revolutions in Milan, Venice, and elsewhere targeted Austrian garrisons. Charles Albert of Sardinia-Piedmont took up arms, hoping to expel Austria from northern Italy.

Failure and Repression

Initially, the revolutions seemed unstoppable. But by 1849, reactionary forces recovered. In Berlin, Frederick William IV rejected the Frankfurt Parliament's crown, unwilling to accept a constitution limiting his prerogatives. Prussian troops dispersed liberal assemblies. Austria suppressed the Hungarian revolution with Russian help, forcibly reasserting Habsburg authority. In Italy, Austrian General Radetzky defeated Charles Albert's army, restoring imperial control in Lombardy-Venetia.

Though the revolutions mostly failed to achieve long-term constitutional democracy, they left important legacies. Some monarchs retained modest liberal reforms; the concept of a unified Germany or Italy did not vanish but instead grew stronger in certain circles. The illusions of a swift liberal triumph gave way to a more strategic approach by nationalist leaders, who realized they needed stronger armies, external allies, or monarchy-based alliances to succeed.

Section III: The Crimean War (1853–1856)

Origins and the Eastern Question

Throughout the 19th century, the **Eastern Question**—the fate of the declining Ottoman Empire—preoccupied European diplomacy. Russia sought to expand its influence in the Balkans and potentially gain access to warm-water ports, while Britain and France feared Russian dominance in the eastern Mediterranean would threaten their trade routes. Austria, wedged between Russia and the Ottoman lands, balanced its own interests carefully.

A dispute over Christian holy places in Jerusalem—then under Ottoman rule—became a flashpoint. Russia claimed to protect Orthodox Christians, while France championed Catholic rights. Ottoman reforms and European rivalries complicated the situation. In 1853, tensions escalated, and Russia occupied the Danubian principalities (Moldavia and Wallachia). The Ottomans declared war, beginning the **Crimean War**.

Coalition Against Russia and the Siege of Sevastopol

Britain and France joined the Ottomans in 1854, seeing an opportunity to contain Russia. Sardinia-Piedmont, eager to gain favor with the western powers for future Italian ambitions, also joined in 1855. Despite initial fighting in the Danubian regions, the primary theater became the Crimean Peninsula, specifically the Russian naval stronghold at **Sevastopol** on the Black Sea.

- **Landing in Crimea**: Allied forces landed near Eupatoria in September 1854, intending to capture Sevastopol. Early battles, like **Alma** (20 September 1854), saw the Russians defeated in open combat.
- **Balaclava and Inkerman**: In October 1854, the **Battle of Balaclava** featured the infamous **Charge of the Light Brigade**, where miscommunication led British cavalry to charge a well-defended Russian position, suffering heavy casualties. The **Battle of Inkerman** (November 1854) was a brutal, fog-shrouded engagement that ended in a Russian retreat.

- **Prolonged Siege**: The Allies laid siege to Sevastopol for almost a year, hampered by inadequate logistics and harsh winters. Disease ravaged both sides. Eventually, the Allies captured vital outworks and forced the Russians to evacuate the city in September 1855.

Diplomatic Outcomes

Tsar Nicholas I died in 1855, succeeded by Alexander II, who sought an end to the costly war. By early 1856, negotiations led to the **Treaty of Paris**. Russia agreed to demilitarize the Black Sea (no warships or naval arsenals) and renounce claims of sole protector of Orthodox Christians in the Ottoman Empire. Although not a total victory for the Allies—Russia remained influential in the region—the war checked immediate Russian expansion. For the Ottomans, the Crimean War offered temporary relief from Russian pressure, but it highlighted the empire's internal weaknesses and dependence on foreign help.

The Crimean War also exposed the inefficiency of many armies. Britain's logistical failures, revealed by war correspondents like William Howard Russell, prompted major reforms in military administration and health (Florence Nightingale's role in improving hospital conditions became legendary). The conflict thus accelerated modernization in the armed forces of several countries.

Section IV: The Wars of Italian Unification (1848–1870)

Background and Key Players

After the failed 1848 revolutions, Italian patriots realized that unification under a moderate constitutional monarchy might be more viable than purely republican uprisings. The Kingdom of Sardinia-Piedmont, ruled by the **House of Savoy**, became the driving force for **Italian unification**—the **Risorgimento**. Prime Minister **Count Camillo di Cavour** skillfully pursued alliances, industrial growth, and diplomatic cunning. Meanwhile, revolutionaries like **Giuseppe Garibaldi** championed popular involvement, leading volunteer forces in the field.

Second War of Italian Independence (1859)

Cavour recognized that Sardinia-Piedmont alone could not defeat Austria (which still controlled Lombardy-Venetia). He sought an alliance with France's **Napoleon**

III, promising the cession of Savoy and Nice to France if Italy were liberated from Austrian rule. Tensions with Austria escalated, and in 1859, Austria delivered an ultimatum that triggered war.

- **Franco-Piedmontese Success**: French armies joined Piedmontese forces in Lombardy. Key battles included **Magenta** (4 June 1859) and **Solferino** (24 June 1859). While the Allies prevailed, the fighting was bloody and disorganized, prompting humanitarian concerns. (Henri Dunant's experience at Solferino later inspired the creation of the Red Cross.)
- **Armistice and Territorial Gains**: Napoleon III, disturbed by the carnage and wary of Prussian mobilization, abruptly signed an armistice with Austria at **Villafranca**. Piedmont gained Lombardy but not Venetia. Still, several central Italian duchies joined Sardinia-Piedmont through plebiscites, expanding the new state significantly.

Garibaldi's Expedition of the Thousand (1860–1861)

While Cavour consolidated northern and central Italy, **Giuseppe Garibaldi** launched a bold expedition to southern Italy with about 1,000 red-shirted volunteers. Landing in Sicily, he overthrew the Bourbon Kingdom of the Two Sicilies, capturing Naples by September 1860. Fearing Garibaldi's radical leanings, Cavour rushed Piedmontese armies south to ensure that unification proceeded under the Savoy monarchy, not a republican revolution.

By early 1861, most of the peninsula, except Rome (controlled by the Pope with French protection) and Venetia (still Austrian), recognized King **Vittorio Emanuele II** as monarch of a unified Italy. Garibaldi ceded his conquests to the new kingdom, enabling the official proclamation of the **Kingdom of Italy** in March 1861.

Third War of Italian Independence (1866) and the Capture of Rome (1870)

In 1866, Italy allied with Prussia against Austria in the **Austro-Prussian War**. Although Italy suffered defeats at **Custoza** and **Lissa**, the Prussian victory forced Austria to relinquish Venetia to the Italians. The final piece, **Rome**, fell after the withdrawal of French garrison troops during the **Franco-Prussian War** (1870–1871). Italian forces occupied Rome in September 1870, making it the capital of the kingdom. Hence, by 1871, Italy's unification was essentially complete—a patchwork of once-divided states now joined in a single monarchy.

Section V: The Franco-Prussian War (1870–1871)

Tensions Between France and Prussia

As Italy moved toward unity, a parallel transformation unfolded in the German states. After the Austro-Prussian War of 1866, **Prussia**, led by **Otto von Bismarck**, excluded Austria from German affairs and formed the **North German Confederation**. Bismarck sought further unification of southern German states under Prussian leadership. Meanwhile, France's Emperor Napoleon III, seeing a strong Prussia as a threat, looked for ways to halt German consolidation.

A diplomatic quarrel over the candidacy of a Hohenzollern prince to the Spanish throne sparked a crisis. Bismarck manipulated communications—the famous **Ems Dispatch**—to inflame French public opinion. On 19 July 1870, France declared war on Prussia, expecting a short, victorious conflict. Bismarck used the declaration to rally the southern German states (Bavaria, Württemberg, Baden) alongside Prussia in a patriotic defense.

Military Campaigns

- **Early Battles**: Prussia's General Helmuth von Moltke organized rapid mobilization via efficient railways and advanced staff planning. The combined German armies outnumbered and outmaneuvered the French. In August 1870, battles at **Wörth**, **Spicheren**, and **Mars-la-Tour** ended in French retreats.
- **Sedan**: The crucial engagement occurred on 1 September 1870 at **Sedan**, where the Germans encircled the main French army. Emperor Napoleon III personally surrendered with 100,000 troops. This catastrophic defeat ended the Second Empire.
- **Siege of Paris**: Following Sedan, a new French government (the Third Republic) continued resistance, but German forces laid siege to Paris. Despite attempts at breakouts and the formation of fresh French armies, the capital endured bombardment and severe shortages. In January 1871, Paris capitulated.

German Empire Proclaimed

During the siege of Paris, the southern German princes consented to unify with the North German Confederation under the Prussian king. On **18 January 1871**, in the Hall of Mirrors at the Palace of Versailles—symbolically chosen to humble France—King **Wilhelm I** of Prussia was proclaimed **German Emperor**. This event crowned Bismarck's plan for a unified German Reich, fundamentally altering Europe's balance of power.

Aftermath and the Paris Commune

France signed the **Treaty of Frankfurt** in May 1871, ceding **Alsace-Lorraine** to the new German Empire and agreeing to pay a heavy indemnity. The war's humiliating outcome fueled bitterness in France toward Germany. Meanwhile, discontent with the conservative Third Republic spurred a radical uprising in Paris: the **Paris Commune** (March–May 1871), a brief socialist experiment crushed by republican troops, leaving thousands dead. The Franco-Prussian War thus ended with Germany ascendant and France grappling with deep internal divisions.

Section VI: Broader Implications of 19th-Century Conflicts

Nationalism as a Driving Force

From the Greek uprising against Ottoman rule to the unifications of Italy and Germany, **nationalism** emerged as a defining ideology. It overrode the conservative spirit of the post-Napoleonic settlement, inspiring movements to form states along linguistic or cultural lines. Even when suppressed (as in the 1848 revolutions), nationalism kept resurfacing until newly unified nations carved out places on the European map.

Decline of Old Empires

The Ottoman Empire, once formidable, struggled to retain its Balkan territories in the face of rising nationalist aspirations (Greece, Serbia, Romania, Bulgaria), as well as encroachments by great powers. The Austrian Empire similarly faced growing internal nationalism from Hungarians, Czechs, Italians, and others, leading eventually to the Ausgleich of 1867, which created the **Austro-Hungarian dual monarchy**. By 1871, the Holy Roman Empire was definitively replaced by a strong German Empire.

New Military Technologies and Methods

Each 19th-century conflict contributed to modernizing warfare. The Crimean War showcased the importance of railways, steamships, and the telegraph. The Franco-Prussian War revealed the impact of quick mobilization and breech-loading rifles, plus the power of heavy artillery. Armies recognized that victory depended on industrial capacity, advanced weaponry, and efficient logistical networks—foreshadowing the total wars of the 20th century.

Realpolitik and Alliances

Diplomacy in this era increasingly embraced **Realpolitik**, a pragmatic approach epitomized by Bismarck. Instead of relying on moral or ideological stances, states sought alliances and treaties purely to advance national interests. The Crimean War saw ephemeral coalitions form around balancing power in Eastern Europe. Italian unification owed much to Cavour's cunning alliance with Napoleon III. The Franco-Prussian War was similarly triggered by carefully orchestrated diplomatic manipulations. This pattern of shifting alliances would later reemerge in the lead-up to World War I.

Section VII: Conclusion

From the Greek War of Independence through the Franco-Prussian War, the 19th century witnessed a succession of conflicts that eroded the conservative framework laid out at the Congress of Vienna in 1815. Each war revealed the growing potency of nationalism, liberal reforms, and industrial technology, even as traditional empires tried to maintain their grip on power. In Southeastern Europe, Greece pioneered a successful national uprising, prompting changes in how great powers approached the "Eastern Question." In Central Europe, repeated revolutions failed initially, but they sparked significant rearrangements, culminating in the creation of Italy and Germany as unified nation-states. Meanwhile, the Crimean War shook the old alliances, introducing new fault lines and underscoring the importance of modern logistics and weaponry.

The **Franco-Prussian War** concluded the long process of German unification and drastically altered Europe's balance of power, with a strong German Empire now dominating the continent. France's defeat generated resentment that would linger for decades. The 19th century thus ended with tensions poised to escalate, as newly formed nations sought their place under the sun, older empires struggled with restive minorities, and alliances formed or shifted according to Realpolitik. As we move into our next chapter, we will broaden our scope further, examining the colonial struggles and intensifying nationalism that characterized the latter part of the 19th century—an era in which European powers projected their rivalries across Africa, Asia, and beyond, setting the stage for further transformations and, ultimately, the path toward the massive conflicts of the 20th century.

Chapter 18: The Wars of the 19th Century — Colonial Struggles and Rising Nationalism

Introduction

While Europe was reshaping itself through major conflicts like the Crimean War and the Franco-Prussian War, another set of wars unfolded on a more global scale. The late 19th century became a period of **imperial expansion**—commonly known as the "Scramble for Africa," along with heightened competition in Asia and other regions. Driven by economic needs (for raw materials and new markets), national prestige, and a belief in European "civilizing missions," the great powers carried out **colonial conquests** and engaged in smaller-scale but often brutal wars against local forces.

Simultaneously, **rising nationalism** affected not only Europe but also regions under foreign domination or heavy influence. Movements of self-determination emerged, challenging old colonial masters or multi-ethnic empires. In this chapter, we will explore how wars in Africa, Asia, and the Americas shaped the 19th-century world—focusing on major conflicts such as the **Opium Wars** in China, the **Anglo-Zulu War** and other African campaigns, the **Indian Rebellion of 1857**, and the role of nationalism in forging or fracturing states. We will also consider the **American Civil War**, a monumental conflict that redefined the United States and influenced future notions of industrialized warfare. By examining these struggles, we see how the 19th century's wars were not confined to Europe's stage but spanned continents, with lasting effects that echoed well into the 20th century.

Section I: The American Civil War (1861–1865)

Causes and Background

Although largely separate from the European power struggles, the **American Civil War** had global significance due to its scale, industrial methods, and the moral-political questions at its core. The United States had grown rapidly, but tensions between free northern states and slaveholding southern states escalated over issues such as states' rights and the expansion of slavery into new territories. The election of **Abraham Lincoln** (1860), who opposed the spread of slavery, triggered **secession** by eleven southern states, forming the **Confederate States of America** under President Jefferson Davis.

Industrialized Warfare

Fighting broke out in April 1861 when Confederate forces bombarded **Fort Sumter** in Charleston Harbor. Both sides mobilized armies in unprecedented numbers—eventually over two million men served in the Union army and roughly 800,000 in the Confederate ranks. The war introduced aspects of modern conflict:

- **Railroads** for rapid troop movement and supply.
- **Telegraphs** for communication.
- **Ironclad warships**, as seen in the duel between USS Monitor and CSS Virginia (1862).
- **Rifled muskets and mass-produced arms**, increasing lethality.

Major battles (Manassas/Bull Run, Antietam, Gettysburg, Vicksburg) caused enormous casualties. By 1862–1863, the Union's industrial might and naval blockade slowly strangled the Confederacy's economy. Lincoln's **Emancipation Proclamation** (1863) turned the conflict into a moral crusade against slavery, discouraging European intervention on the Confederacy's behalf.

Outcome and Impact

The Confederacy collapsed in April 1865 with General Robert E. Lee's surrender at **Appomattox Court House**. The war cost over 600,000–700,000 lives—more American deaths than in any other conflict in U.S. history up to that point. Slavery was abolished, and federal authority over states was confirmed. In global terms, the Civil War underscored the effectiveness of industrial power in warfare, foreshadowing patterns European nations would adopt in future conflicts. It also ended any immediate hopes of splitting the United States into multiple states, allowing a newly reconstituted nation to emerge as a potential world power in the late 19th and early 20th centuries.

Section II: The Opium Wars and Western Expansion in Asia

The First Opium War (1839–1842)

While the American Civil War raged in the 1860s, earlier decades saw significant conflicts elsewhere. In **China**, the **Qing Dynasty** had restricted European trade to a single port at Canton (Guangzhou), limiting foreign merchants' activities. The British East India Company sought to balance its trade deficit by exporting **opium** (grown in British India) to China. When Qing authorities cracked down on the illegal opium trade—confiscating and destroying large opium stocks—Britain responded militarily, initiating the **First Opium War**.

- **Gunboat Diplomacy**: The British navy, equipped with steam-powered warships and modern artillery, quickly defeated Chinese coastal defenses.
- **Treaty of Nanking (1842)**: China was forced to cede **Hong Kong** to Britain, open several treaty ports to foreign trade, and grant extraterritorial rights to British subjects. This "unequal treaty" system undermined Chinese sovereignty, fueling domestic unrest.

The Second Opium War (1856–1860)

Tensions flared again when British and French forces sought further commercial privileges. The **Arrow Incident** (1856) involving a Chinese inspection of a British-registered ship provided a pretext for renewed hostilities. France joined Britain, using a missionary's murder as justification.

- **War and the Sack of the Summer Palaces**: Allied troops marched on Beijing, eventually capturing the city. They **looted and burned** the Old Summer Palace (Yuanmingyuan), an act widely condemned even among some Western observers.
- **Treaties of Tianjin (1858) and Convention of Beijing (1860)**: China had to open more ports, legalize the opium trade, allow foreign legations in Beijing, and grant further concessions. These humiliations deepened the Qing Dynasty's crisis, contributing to internal rebellions like the Taiping Rebellion.

The Opium Wars exemplified Western powers' growing dominance in Asia and the use of superior naval and military technology to compel trade concessions.

They also set a pattern of **"unequal treaties"** that Japan, Korea, and others would soon face, shaping regional geopolitics into the 20th century.

Section III: African Conquests and Resistance

The Scramble for Africa

Europe's industrial powers—Britain, France, Germany, Belgium, Italy, Portugal—sought colonies in Africa to secure raw materials (rubber, ivory, minerals) and new markets. The "Scramble for Africa" accelerated after the **Berlin Conference** (1884–1885), which laid ground rules for partitioning the continent. Colonial expansion often entailed **wars of conquest** against local kingdoms and communities.

- **Anglo-Zulu War (1879)**: In southern Africa, the British sought to dominate the Zulu Kingdom after earlier conflicts in the region. Initially, the Zulus inflicted a shocking defeat on the British at **Isandlwana** (22 January 1879), wiping out a large British force. Yet Britain regrouped, deploying reinforcements and more advanced weaponry, eventually defeating the Zulus and annexing their territory.
- **Mahdist War in Sudan (1881–1899)**: The Sudanese Mahdi, Muhammad Ahmad, led a jihad against Egyptian (and thus British) control. Initially, the Mahdists captured Khartoum (1885), killing British General Gordon. Later, Anglo-Egyptian forces under Kitchener reconquered Sudan (1898), culminating in the **Battle of Omdurman**, demonstrating modern firepower (machine guns, artillery) against Mahdist warriors.
- **Italian-Ethiopian Conflict**: Ethiopia remained one of the few African states to resist colonization effectively. At the **Battle of Adwa (1896)**, Emperor Menelik II's army decisively defeated an Italian invasion, preserving Ethiopia's sovereignty and humiliating Italy's colonial ambitions.

War Tactics and African Agency

Though often overshadowed by the scale of European warfare, African campaigns were significant for their brutality and local complexities. African polities sometimes tried diplomacy or alliances to counter Europeans, while others adapted firearms or used guerrilla tactics. Despite heroic resistance in many regions, European technological superiority (Maxim guns, modern rifles) and internal African rivalries often tipped the balance. The colonial conquest was not universally completed by 1900, but the late 19th century saw large swaths of Africa carved into European empires.

Section IV: The Indian Rebellion of 1857

East India Company Rule

In India, the **British East India Company** had steadily expanded its control since the 18th century, defeating local rulers (nawabs, rajahs) and annexing territories. By mid-19th century, the Company governed vast regions, using local troops called **sepoys** under British officers. Resentment grew among Indian princes who lost sovereignty, landowners stripped of estates, and soldiers facing changes in pay or social practices. Cultural grievances also arose: Christian missionaries, new legal codes, and rumors of forced conversion stirred hostility.

Spark and Spread of Revolt

In 1857, sepoys in Meerut mutinied over new rifle cartridges rumored to be greased with cow and pig fat—offensive to both Hindus and Muslims. The revolt swiftly spread across northern and central India, with sepoys capturing Delhi and proclaiming the aged Mughal emperor, Bahadur Shah II, as a symbolic figurehead. Other centers of resistance included Kanpur, Lucknow, and Jhansi. However, not all parts of India joined the rebellion, and many Indian states sided with the British.

Brutal Suppression and Aftermath

The conflict saw atrocities on both sides. The rebels killed British civilians, including women and children, fueling calls for vengeance in Britain. British reprisals were ruthless, executing suspected rebels and conducting harsh reprisals against entire villages. Gradually, British reinforcements arrived, retaking Delhi and crushing major rebel strongholds. By 1858, the rebellion collapsed.

The British government abolished the East India Company's rule, placing India under direct Crown authority. The **British Raj** was established, with Queen Victoria proclaimed **Empress of India** in 1877. Reforms tried to address some grievances, but overall, the Raj system deepened Britain's direct exploitation of India. The rebellion also stirred early nationalist sentiments among Indians, planting seeds for future independence movements.

Section V: Other Late 19th-Century Conflicts in Asia and Beyond

The Taiping Rebellion (1850–1864)

While not strictly a colonial war, China's **Taiping Rebellion** overlapped with Western interventions. A Christian-influenced leader, Hong Xiuquan, proclaimed himself the brother of Jesus and led a massive revolt against the Qing Dynasty. Taiping insurgents captured Nanjing, threatening to overthrow the Qing. The rebellion caused tens of millions of deaths, making it one of history's deadliest conflicts. Qing loyalist armies, aided by European arms and sometimes foreign advisers (like "Ever Victorious Army" under Frederick Townsend Ward and Charles Gordon), eventually crushed the Taipings. This enormous civil war weakened China further, exposing it to more foreign pressures and setting the stage for later uprisings (e.g., the Boxer Rebellion of 1900).

French Expansion in Southeast Asia

France, which had already established a foothold in Algeria (starting in 1830), turned to Indochina (Vietnam, Cambodia, Laos). Initially pursuing missionary protection, France escalated to outright conquests:

- **Cochinchina Campaigns (1858–1862)**: French forces seized control of southern Vietnam, forming the colony of Cochinchina.
- **Subsequent Conflicts**: By the 1880s and 1890s, France extended protectorates over Annam, Tonkin, and Cambodia, culminating in the **French Indochina** union. Local resistance was constant, but French firepower and political maneuvers prevailed.

The Opening of Japan and Internal Strife

Japan, relatively isolated under the Tokugawa Shogunate for centuries, faced "gunboat diplomacy" from the United States in 1853, when Commodore Matthew Perry demanded trade access. European powers soon followed, leading to unequal treaties that undermined Japanese sovereignty. This period of humiliation spurred internal movements to overthrow the shogunate (the **Meiji Restoration** of 1868), modernize the state, and build a strong military to resist Western colonization. Although not a major 19th-century war with Europeans, Japan's transformation set it on a path to become an imperial power itself, as seen in the Sino-Japanese War of 1894–1895 (beyond our immediate scope).

Section VI: Late 19th-Century Nationalism and State-Building

Balkan Nationalism After Greek Independence

Following Greece's successful revolt, other Balkan peoples under Ottoman rule pursued independence or autonomy. The 19th century saw uprisings by **Serbians, Romanians, Bulgarians**, and others. Russia often supported these movements as part of its pan-Slavic policy, while Austria-Hungary feared the spread of Slavic nationalism within its own borders. The resulting tensions contributed to the tinderbox environment that would eventually ignite in 1914, but the seeds were sown in these smaller 19th-century conflicts, often overshadowed by larger wars.

The Dual Monarchy in Austria-Hungary

Defeats in 1859 (by France and Sardinia-Piedmont) and 1866 (by Prussia) forced Austria to compromise with its largest ethnic minority, the Hungarians. The **Ausgleich (Compromise) of 1867** created Austria-Hungary, giving Hungary its own legislature and significant autonomy while sharing a common emperor (Franz Joseph I), foreign policy, and military. This arrangement calmed Magyar discontent but left other ethnic groups—Czechs, Slavs, Romanians, Italians—still unhappy. Internal frictions endured, hinting at future crises.

North and South America

Beyond the American Civil War, other conflicts shaped the Western Hemisphere. In South America, wars of independence in the early 19th century had produced new republics. Post-independence struggles included **caudillo** rule, civil wars, and boundary disputes. For example, the **War of the Triple Alliance (1864–1870)** pitted Paraguay against Brazil, Argentina, and Uruguay—a devastating conflict that nearly annihilated Paraguay's male population. Meanwhile, in Mexico, the **French intervention (1862–1867)** installed Archduke Maximilian of Austria as emperor, but liberal forces under Benito Juárez eventually defeated the French-backed regime.

Section VII: Patterns and Consequences of 19th-Century Colonial Wars

Military Disparities and Local Resistance

In Africa and Asia, Western powers leveraged industrial advantages—steamships, railways, repeating rifles, machine guns—to subdue local polities. Resistance varied: some leaders attempted modernization (e.g., Ethiopia's Menelik II), others tried alliances or sought foreign patrons. Although often outgunned, indigenous forces sometimes scored notable victories or prolonged campaigns, undermining illusions of easy conquest. Still, by the close of the 19th century, most of Africa and large parts of Asia were under direct European rule or heavy influence.

Economic and Societal Effects

Colonial wars reshaped global trade. European powers extracted raw materials—cotton, rubber, minerals—from colonies, fueling industrial production at home. In turn, colonized regions saw disruptions to traditional economies, forced labor systems, and new forms of exploitation (e.g., Congo Free State under King Leopold II). Missionaries and administrators introduced Western education, Christianity, and infrastructure, but these often served colonial interests more than local development. Over time, colonial subjects formed new identities, combining indigenous cultures with Western ideas, eventually giving rise to nationalist movements in the 20th century.

Section VIII: The Road Toward the 20th Century

By the late 19th century, the map of the world had changed dramatically due to colonial expansion, the rise of newly unified states like Italy and Germany, and the continuing decline of older empires like the Ottoman or Qing. Nationalism had proven a formidable force, fueling both independence movements and imperial conquests. Meanwhile, Europe's great powers hammered out **spheres of influence** overseas, competing for prestige and resources, forging alliances that sometimes served as tinder for future conflicts.

Military technology raced ahead, from muzzle-loaded muskets to breech-loading rifles and early machine guns, while railroad networks and steam navies revolutionized logistics. Wars like the American Civil War showed that industrial might could determine victory, an omen for the massive industrial conflicts to come. Warfare's scale and intensity grew, and armies no longer relied on small professional forces but on conscription-based mass armies, reflecting the broadening involvement of entire societies in conflict.

These developments set the stage for the largest conflicts in the 20th century. While the powers strove to maintain a balance, suspicion and rivalry ran high—particularly after Germany's unification in 1871 shifted Europe's power dynamic. Colonial entanglements, economic competition, arms races, and nationalist fervor all coalesced into a precarious environment that would ultimately implode in 1914. But that next phase—World War I—lies beyond our current scope, as we have focused on the 19th century's wars that bridged the Napoleonic era and the modern world.

Conclusion

Throughout the 19th century, conflicts extended well beyond Europe's Napoleonic transformations. In this chapter, we examined how **colonial struggles**, **rising nationalism**, and **modernizing militaries** reshaped large parts of the globe. Wars like the **Opium Wars** in China exposed the vulnerability of ancient empires to Western technology, inaugurating a period of semi-colonial entanglements that would last until the mid-20th century. The **Scramble for Africa** replaced older African kingdoms and societies with European colonial regimes, often enforced through brutal warfare. In India, the **1857 Rebellion** ended East India Company rule but tightened Britain's direct grip. Meanwhile, the **American Civil War** redefined the trajectory of the United States, pioneering industrial-scale warfare that would inspire future conflicts.

Nationalism remained the key factor linking these disparate wars. Whether driving unification in Italy and Germany, fueling independence movements in Greece or Latin America, or underpinning anti-colonial resistance, the concept of a people united by language, culture, or shared identity rapidly gained momentum. As we close the 19th century's chapter on global warfare, the seeds of the 20th century's vast upheavals are firmly planted—great powers on edge, newly armed with advanced technology, ruling vast colonial empires, and contending with restless subject peoples. In the next installments of our historical survey, we will see how these tensions erupted into even larger conflagrations, forever altering the course of world history.

Chapter 19: World War I

Introduction

World War I, often called the **Great War**, lasted from 1914 to 1918. It was one of the deadliest and most transformative wars up to that point in human history, involving nations from across the globe. Though fighting was centered in Europe, colonial empires drew in soldiers and resources from Africa, Asia, and beyond. This conflict introduced trench warfare on a massive scale, saw the first large-scale use of modern weapons like tanks and airplanes, and led to the downfall of empires that had ruled for centuries.

In this chapter, we will explore the long and short-term causes of World War I, the course of the fighting on various fronts, the impact on soldiers and civilians, and the final outcomes that set the stage for future conflicts. By the end of 1918, the map of Europe was redrawn, entire societies were traumatized, and a fragile peace was established—one that ultimately failed to prevent a second global war just two decades later. Nevertheless, World War I stands as a pivotal turning point in the story of modern warfare, reshaping how armies fought and how citizens perceived the nature of total war.

Section I: Seeds of Conflict and the Alliance System

1. **Long-Term Causes**
    - **Nationalism**: By the early 20th century, many European nations were driven by strong nationalist sentiments. Some ethnic groups, like Slavs under Austro-Hungarian rule, desired independence. Established powers like France and Germany nurtured nationalist pride that fueled competition.
    - **Imperial Rivalries**: Nations such as Britain, France, and Germany vied for global colonies, seeking raw materials and markets for their growing industries. Competition in Africa and Asia heightened tensions.
    - **Militarism**: Germany, Great Britain, and others expanded their navies and armies. Military leaders gained influence in governments, encouraging the belief that war could be quick and decisive.

- **Entangling Alliances**: Europe split into major blocs. The **Triple Entente** of France, Russia, and Britain stood opposite the **Triple Alliance** of Germany, Austria-Hungary, and Italy. Although Italy initially allied with Germany and Austria-Hungary, it later switched sides during the war.

2. **The Powder Keg of the Balkans**
    - The Balkans was an especially volatile region. The Ottoman Empire's decline left a power vacuum, and local nationalisms clashed.
    - Serbia, supported by Russia, sought to unite South Slavs, challenging Austria-Hungary's control over diverse groups in Bosnia-Herzegovina and beyond.
    - This tension meant any local crisis might spark a broader confrontation, given that larger powers had pledged to protect their allies' interests.

3. **Immediate Spark: Assassination in Sarajevo**
    - On 28 June 1914, Archduke Franz Ferdinand of Austria-Hungary was assassinated in Sarajevo by a Bosnian Serb nationalist, Gavrilo Princip.
    - Austria-Hungary blamed Serbia for supporting militant groups. Backed by German "blank check" assurances, Austria-Hungary issued an ultimatum to Serbia.
    - Diplomatic efforts failed. Austria-Hungary declared war on Serbia, prompting Russia to mobilize in Serbia's defense. Germany declared war on Russia and France, while Britain joined once Belgium's neutrality was violated. The network of alliances turned a regional crisis into a continental war.

Section II: Military Strategies and the Opening Moves

4. **War Plans and Early Expectations**
    - Germany's **Schlieffen Plan** aimed to avoid a two-front war by defeating France rapidly (via Belgium) before turning east against Russia.
    - France's strategy (Plan XVII) involved a direct offensive into Alsace-Lorraine, hoping for a swift victory to reclaim lost provinces from the Franco-Prussian War.

- Russia's vast size suggested slow mobilization, but leaders believed sheer numbers could pressure Germany.
- Britain's small but professional **British Expeditionary Force (BEF)** crossed to France to halt German advances.

5. **The Western Front: Race to the Sea**
    - Germany's invasion of Belgium in August 1914 encountered stronger resistance than expected. The German advance toward Paris was eventually halted at the **First Battle of the Marne** (September 1914), where Franco-British forces prevented a quick German victory.
    - Both sides then tried outflanking each other in northern France, leading to the so-called "Race to the Sea." By late 1914, continuous trench lines stretched from the Swiss border to the North Sea.

6. **Eastern Front and Other Theaters**
    - Russia advanced into East Prussia and Galicia, initially surprising the Germans. However, Germany's generals Hindenburg and Ludendorff inflicted heavy defeats on the Russians at **Tannenberg** and the **Masurian Lakes** in 1914.
    - Austria-Hungary struggled against both Russia and Serbia, suffering major setbacks in the Carpathians. Meanwhile, the Ottoman Empire entered the war on Germany's side, threatening the Russian Caucasus region and facing British campaigns in Mesopotamia (Iraq) and Palestine.

Section III: The Stalemate and Trench Warfare

7. **Life in the Trenches**
    - By 1915, the Western Front devolved into **trench warfare**, with opposing armies dug into fortified lines. Trenches were muddy, rat-infested, and disease-ridden. Soldiers faced artillery barrages, snipers, and poison gas attacks.
    - "No Man's Land," the area between enemy trenches, was strewn with barbed wire, shell craters, and corpses, making direct assaults extremely costly.

8. **New Weapons and Tactics**
    - **Machine Guns**: Rapid-fire weapons inflicted massive casualties on attacking infantry.

- **Poison Gas**: First used by Germany at Ypres in 1915, gas spread fear and horrible injuries. Soon, all sides developed chemical munitions (chlorine, phosgene, mustard gas) and gas masks.
- **Heavy Artillery**: Huge guns caused most battlefield casualties, constantly bombarding enemy lines.
- **Tanks**: Introduced by Britain in 1916, tanks tried to break the stalemate, but early models were unreliable. Over time, tanks improved and became a vital tool.
- **Airpower**: Airplanes initially served for reconnaissance; later, they carried bombs and engaged in "dogfights." Though limited, they hinted at the future role of air warfare.

9. **Failed Offensives**
   - Generals on both sides believed large offensives might deliver a breakthrough. Battles like **Neuve Chapelle** (1915), the **Second Battle of Ypres** (1915), and **Loos** ended in heavy casualties with minimal territorial gain.
   - The Eastern Front remained fluid compared to the West, but Russia's initial momentum faded due to shortages in weapons, leadership problems, and enormous casualty rates.

Section IV: 1916–1917: Slaughter, Attrition, and Shifting Momentum

10. **Verdun and the Somme (1916)**
- The **Battle of Verdun** (February–December 1916) was a massive German attempt to "bleed France white." The French, under General Pétain, held their ground despite horrendous losses. Both sides suffered over half a million casualties.
- On the **Somme** (July–November 1916), British and French forces attacked German lines. The first day alone saw nearly 60,000 British casualties. After months of fighting, little ground was gained, but the battle highlighted the slow shift toward more sophisticated artillery barrages and creeping barrages. Despite this, casualties soared into the hundreds of thousands.

11. **Naval Warfare and the War at Sea**
- Britain's **Grand Fleet** blockaded Germany, causing shortages in food and raw materials. Germany retaliated with **U-boats** (submarines), threatening Allied shipping.

- The **Battle of Jutland** (31 May–1 June 1916) was the main clash of battleships in the North Sea. Although tactically inconclusive, Britain retained naval dominance, continuing the blockade. Germany's surface fleet remained mostly inactive afterward, relying instead on U-boat warfare.

12. **Diplomatic Developments and the War's Global Scale**
- In 1915, Italy switched to the Allied side, hoping to gain Austrian territory. Italian offensives along the Isonzo River resulted in bloody stalemates.
- The Ottoman Empire battled in the Middle East, facing a British-led campaign in Palestine and the Arab Revolt (aided by T. E. Lawrence). The **Gallipoli Campaign** (1915–1916), aimed at knocking the Ottomans out of the war, ended in disaster for the Allies.
- Japan, allied with Britain, seized German colonies in the Pacific. Meanwhile, Germany supported revolts in Ireland (the 1916 Easter Rising) and among Muslims under British rule, attempting to destabilize the Allies.

13. **Russia's Exit and America's Entry (1917)**
- By 1917, Russia was collapsing under war strains. The **February Revolution** toppled the Tsar, and continued battlefield failures led to the **October Revolution**, wherein the Bolsheviks seized power. They signed the **Treaty of Brest-Litovsk (March 1918)** with Germany, exiting the war and ceding vast territories.
- Germany's decision to resume **unrestricted submarine warfare** in early 1917, sinking neutral shipping (including American vessels), along with the **Zimmermann Telegram** fiasco (a German proposal for Mexico to attack the US) pushed President Woodrow Wilson to declare war on Germany in April 1917. American troops would take time to arrive, but their entry transformed the balance of manpower and resources.

Section V: The Endgame of World War I (1918)

14. **German Spring Offensives**
- Freed from the Eastern Front, Germany launched major attacks in spring 1918 on the Western Front, hoping to deliver a knockout blow before American forces fully deployed. Stormtrooper tactics broke Allied lines initially.

- However, Allied defenses stiffened, and the offensives ran out of momentum due to supply issues and high German casualties. Fresh American divisions arrived in large numbers, boosting Allied morale.

15. **Allied Counterattack**
- The Allies, now under unified command led by France's Marshal Foch, counterattacked in mid-1918. Battles like **Amiens** (August 1918) showed the power of combined arms—tanks, artillery, infantry, and aircraft coordinating to roll back German positions.
- Germany's political and economic situation deteriorated. Starvation, strikes, and growing discontent made continuing the war untenable. Allied forces pressed on toward German borders.

16. **Collapse of Central Powers**
- Bulgaria, the Ottoman Empire, and Austria-Hungary all sought armistices in autumn 1918 as Allied offensives overwhelmed them. Internal revolutions erupted in Austria-Hungary; Emperor Karl found himself powerless to hold the empire together.
- Germany's Kaiser Wilhelm II abdicated on 9 November 1918 amid uprisings at home. The new republican government accepted an **armistice** that took effect at **11 a.m. on 11 November 1918**, ending the fighting on the Western Front.

Section VI: Consequences and Legacy

17. **Human Cost and Psychological Impact**
- Approximately 9 to 10 million soldiers died, with countless more wounded. Civilian deaths due to famine and disease also soared, especially in the Ottoman domains and Eastern Europe.
- The scale of the carnage shook societies, leading to cynicism and what came to be called the "Lost Generation." Monuments and war cemeteries became reminders of the colossal sacrifice.

18. **Redrawing the Map**
- The **Treaty of Versailles (1919)** forced Germany to accept blame, pay reparations, and reduce its army. Germany also lost territory to Poland, France, and others. New states arose from the Austro-Hungarian, Russian, and Ottoman empires: Czechoslovakia, Yugoslavia, Finland, Estonia, Latvia, Lithuania, and others.

- The war ended dynasties: the Hohenzollerns in Germany, the Habsburgs in Austria-Hungary, the Romanovs in Russia, and the Ottomans in Turkey. A fragile democracy replaced them in many cases, but the seeds of future turmoil were planted.

19. **League of Nations**
- President Wilson championed the **League of Nations** as a means to prevent future conflicts through collective security and diplomacy. However, the United States Senate refused to ratify the treaty, so the US never joined. Weakened by absence of major powers and a lack of enforcement mechanisms, the League faced serious challenges.

20. **Prelude to Another War**
- Although the Great War was called "the war to end all wars," the peace settlements left numerous grievances unaddressed. Germany resented the harsh terms, Italy felt it had not received all it deserved, and Eastern Europe was a patchwork of new states with ethnic tensions. The ideological conflicts also rose: communism in Russia, rising fascism in Italy. Within two decades, these unresolved issues would ignite **World War II**.

Chapter 20: World War II

Introduction

World War II (1939–1945) stands as the deadliest and most expansive conflict in history, involving the major powers and countless smaller nations across Europe, Asia, Africa, and the Pacific. With roots in the aftermath of World War I, the rise of totalitarian regimes in Germany, Italy, and Japan led to policies of aggression and territorial expansion. Democratic states, still scarred by the Great War, were slow to confront these threats, hoping to avoid another catastrophe.

In this final chapter, we will examine the key causes and turning points of World War II, including the role of ideologies like fascism, the major theaters of operation (Europe, North Africa, and the Pacific), the horrific crimes against humanity (most notably the Holocaust), and the war's far-reaching consequences. By 1945, entire continents lay in ruin, marking the end of an era dominated by European imperial powers and paving the way for new global realities. World War II's conclusion would finalize the transformations begun in World War I, shaping a new map of alliances, spheres of influence, and the dawn of the nuclear age.

Section I: Road to War and Axis Ambitions

1. **The Rise of Fascist States**
    - **Nazi Germany**: In 1933, Adolf Hitler came to power, promising to reverse the Versailles Treaty, rebuild Germany's military, and unite all German-speaking peoples. Anti-Semitism and authoritarian rule became state policy.
    - **Fascist Italy**: Benito Mussolini, in power since the early 1920s, invaded Ethiopia in 1935, seeking a "new Roman Empire." The League of Nations failed to stop this aggression.
    - **Imperial Japan**: Militarists aimed to dominate East Asia. Japan occupied Manchuria in 1931 and waged full war on China in 1937, committing atrocities like the Rape of Nanking.
2. **Failure of Appeasement**
    - Britain and France, haunted by memories of World War I, tried to avoid conflict through **appeasement**. They allowed Hitler to

remilitarize the Rhineland (1936), annex Austria (1938), and gain the Sudetenland from Czechoslovakia via the Munich Agreement (1938).
    - Hitler's blatant violation of these pacts, culminating in the occupation of the rest of Czechoslovakia in March 1939, revealed appeasement's failure. Britain and France then pledged to defend Poland if attacked.
3. **Molotov-Ribbentrop Pact**
    - In August 1939, Nazi Germany and the Soviet Union signed a non-aggression treaty, secretly agreeing to split Poland and grant spheres of influence in Eastern Europe. This pact shocked the world, as Germany was staunchly anti-communist. But Hitler sought to avoid a two-front war, while Stalin aimed to buy time for Soviet rearmament.

Section II: The War Begins (1939–1941)

4. **Invasion of Poland and the Phony War**
    - On 1 September 1939, Germany invaded Poland using **Blitzkrieg** tactics—rapid armor thrusts, air support, and encirclement. Britain and France declared war on Germany, but offered little direct assistance to Poland, which fell within weeks.
    - The Soviet Union invaded eastern Poland on 17 September, per the secret deal. By October, Poland was partitioned, with Germany annexing western areas and the Soviets controlling the east.
    - For months, little fighting occurred in the west, leading to the term **"Phony War."** Meanwhile, the Soviets attacked Finland (the Winter War of 1939–1940), eventually forcing concessions.
5. **Blitzkrieg in the West**
    - In April 1940, Germany conquered Denmark and Norway to secure iron ore shipments from Sweden.
    - On 10 May, the Wehrmacht overran the **Low Countries** (Belgium, Netherlands, Luxembourg) and bypassed France's Maginot Line through the Ardennes forest. The speed of Germany's advance trapped Allied forces in Belgium, leading to the **Dunkirk evacuation** (late May to early June 1940), where hundreds of

- thousands of British and French troops escaped across the English Channel.
- Paris fell in June 1940; France signed an armistice, splitting the country into the German-occupied north and the nominally independent **Vichy regime** in the south.

6. **Battle of Britain and the Blitz**
    - Britain under Prime Minister Winston Churchill refused any peace with Hitler. In summer 1940, the Luftwaffe tried to gain air superiority to prepare an invasion (Operation Sea Lion). The **Battle of Britain** saw the Royal Air Force (RAF) repel massive German air raids, thanks to radar, strong fighter tactics (Spitfire, Hurricane), and strategic leadership.
    - Frustrated, Germany shifted to bombing British cities—the **Blitz**—aiming to break morale. Though many civilians died, Britain stood firm, and the invasion plan was shelved.

7. **Mediterranean and Africa**
    - Italy, allied with Germany, attacked Greece and British forces in North Africa. However, the Greek campaign faltered, prompting Germany to aid Italy in the Balkans (April 1941) and seize Yugoslavia.
    - In North Africa, the **Afrika Korps** under General Rommel clashed with British Commonwealth troops. Though Rommel's tactics were bold, supply issues and Allied counterattacks kept the theater in flux.

Section III: Operation Barbarossa and the Globalization of Conflict

8. **Invasion of the Soviet Union (1941)**
    - Despite the non-aggression pact, Hitler's long-term aim was to destroy the Soviet Union and seize its resources. On 22 June 1941, Germany launched **Operation Barbarossa**, the largest invasion in history.
    - Initially, the Soviets were taken by surprise, suffering huge losses. German armies advanced toward Leningrad, Moscow, and Ukraine. However, the Soviet Union's vast distances, harsh winters, and determined resistance prevented a quick German victory.

9. **Pearl Harbor and US Entry**
    - In Asia, Japan continued its war in China and eyed Southeast Asia for resources. The US oil embargo pressured Japan, which decided on a preemptive strike. On 7 December 1941, Japan bombed the US Pacific Fleet at **Pearl Harbor**, Hawaii.
    - The next day, the US declared war on Japan, and Germany declared war on the US, fully globalizing the conflict. The Allies now included the **Big Three**: the US, Britain, and the Soviet Union. Japan's expansions soon stretched across the Pacific, capturing the Philippines, Singapore, and other territories, though fierce resistance remained.
10. **Allied Strategy and Axis Mistakes**
- Germany's advanced lines overstretched. The Soviet winter offensive near Moscow (December 1941) halted the Germans. Siege warfare continued at Leningrad, while Hitler directed a southern push in 1942 to seize oil fields in the Caucasus.
- Japan's early successes drew the US into a two-ocean war, as the US rapidly rebuilt its navy and mobilized industrial capacity. Meanwhile, Italy's campaigns faltered in North Africa and the Balkans. The Axis powers never fully coordinated their strategies, often acting on separate ambitions.

Section IV: Turning the Tide (1942–1943)

11. **Stalingrad and the Eastern Front**
- In mid-1942, the German 6th Army advanced into southern Russia, reaching Stalingrad on the Volga River. This city became a brutal urban battleground from August 1942 to February 1943. The Soviets encircled the 6th Army in November (Operation Uranus), leading to its surrender in early 1943.
- **Stalingrad** marked a major turning point. Germany lost an entire army, and Soviet forces gained confidence, pushing westward in subsequent offensives.
12. **North Africa and the Mediterranean**
- The British 8th Army, under General Montgomery, halted Rommel at **El Alamein** (October–November 1942), then drove the Axis back across Libya.

- Allied landings in **French North Africa** (Operation Torch, November 1942) forced Axis forces into a two-front fight. By May 1943, the Allies cleared Tunisia, capturing large numbers of German and Italian troops.
- Next, the Allies invaded **Sicily** (July 1943) and then Italy's mainland. Mussolini's regime collapsed, and Italy switched sides, though German divisions occupied much of the peninsula, prolonging a hard-fought campaign.

13. **War in the Pacific**
- In the Pacific, Japan's initial momentum stalled at **Midway** (June 1942), where the US Navy sank four Japanese carriers. This major carrier battle shifted naval power to the US.
- The **Guadalcanal** campaign (August 1942–February 1943) was the first major Allied counteroffensive in the Pacific, with brutal fighting on land, sea, and air. Despite heavy losses, the US eventually forced Japan to retreat. An "island-hopping" strategy emerged, bypassing some Japanese strongpoints to strike more strategically vital islands.

Section V: Allied Advance and Axis Collapse (1944–1945)

14. **Strategic Bombing and the Western Front**
- Allied bombers targeted Germany's industrial centers, aiming to cripple war production and morale. British nighttime area bombing and US daytime precision raids devastated cities like Hamburg and Dresden, though critics questioned the moral and strategic value of such destruction.
- On 6 June 1944 (**D-Day**), Allied forces under General Eisenhower landed in Normandy, France (Operation Overlord). The establishment of a Second Front forced Germany to fight in both east and west.
- By August, Paris was liberated, and Allied armies drove toward Germany's western border. A German counterattack in the **Ardennes** (Battle of the Bulge, December 1944) briefly delayed the Allied advance but soon collapsed.

15. **Eastern Front Surge**
- After Stalingrad, the Soviets won further victories at **Kursk** (July 1943)—the largest tank battle in history—and pushed relentlessly westward. By late 1944, Soviet armies had reclaimed most of their

territory and entered Eastern Europe, liberating or occupying countries from the Baltic to the Balkans.
- Germany's allies (Romania, Bulgaria, Hungary) switched sides or were invaded. The Red Army approached Berlin by early 1945.

16. **Defeat of Germany**
- With Allied forces crossing the Rhine in March 1945 and Soviets closing in from the east, Germany's defeat was imminent.
- Hitler, entrenched in his Berlin bunker, refused surrender. Finally, on 30 April 1945, he committed suicide. Berlin fell to Soviet forces. Germany unconditionally surrendered on **8 May 1945** (VE Day—Victory in Europe Day).

17. **The War in the Pacific Endgame**
- As Germany collapsed, the US intensified its fight against Japan. Costly battles at **Iwo Jima** (February–March 1945) and **Okinawa** (April–June 1945) demonstrated Japan's fierce resistance, kamikaze attacks, and heavy civilian toll.
- With invasion of the Japanese home islands looming, the US tested and then used the **atomic bomb** on Hiroshima (6 August 1945) and Nagasaki (9 August 1945). The unprecedented destruction prompted Japan's surrender announcement on 15 August 1945 (VJ Day). Official surrender took place on 2 September 1945.

Section VI: The Holocaust and War Crimes

18. **Nazi Genocide**
- Central to Nazi ideology was the systematic persecution and murder of Jews, Slavs, Romani people, disabled individuals, political dissidents, and others deemed "undesirable."
- The Holocaust took shape as **death camps** like Auschwitz, Treblinka, and Sobibor were built for industrial-scale genocide. Millions of Jews were killed, along with Poles, Soviet POWs, and others.
- Liberation of the camps by Allied troops revealed the full horror, influencing postwar trials and discussions of human rights.

19. **Atrocities Elsewhere**
- Japan's imperial armies committed widespread atrocities in China and Southeast Asia, including the **Nanking Massacre** (1937) and brutal

treatment of POWs, exemplified by the Bataan Death March in the Philippines (1942).
- Mass bombings of civilian areas, from London to Dresden to Tokyo, raised ethical questions about total war tactics. The new extremes of violence forced reexamination of warfare's moral boundaries.

Section VII: Aftermath and Consequences

20. Unprecedented Destruction
- World War II caused upward of 50 million to 60 million deaths globally. Cities lay in ruin, economies shattered, and entire populations displaced.
- In Europe, borders were redrawn, refugees roamed, and countries from Poland to France had to rebuild. Many colonies hoped postwar promises of self-determination would lead to independence.
- In Asia, China was devastated, and Japanese-held territories changed hands. The bombings of Hiroshima and Nagasaki introduced the nuclear age, overshadowing any prior scale of destructive power.

21. Formation of the United Nations
- Determined to prevent another global catastrophe, Allied leaders planned a new international body—the **United Nations (UN)**. It replaced the League of Nations, aiming to improve collective security and foster cooperation.
- The **UN Charter** was signed in June 1945, even before the war ended in the Pacific. While not eliminating power rivalries, the UN provided a forum for dialogue and set forth ideals of human rights.

22. Shifts in Global Power
- The war's end saw the decline of old imperial powers: Britain and France were economically weakened, their colonies increasingly seeking independence. The battered Soviet Union emerged as a superpower controlling Eastern Europe. The United States, relatively unscathed at home, became the world's largest economy and a major military force.
- Germany was partitioned, and Japan was occupied by the US. Italy overthrew Mussolini's regime. The global center of gravity moved away from Western Europe to a new bipolar system overshadowed by the US and the USSR.

23. Long Shadow of the War
- The massive devastation gave rise to new institutions and multilateral agreements, such as the **International Military Tribunal at Nuremberg**

to prosecute Nazi war criminals, and later the **Geneva Conventions** updates on humane treatment in war.
- World War II's conclusion marked the end of this volume's coverage but laid the seeds for future geopolitical tensions, including the division of Europe, the Cold War, and decolonization struggles across Africa and Asia.

Conclusion

World War II surpassed all previous conflicts in scale, casualties, and the depth of its impact. Its total nature merged military and civilian targets, introduced nuclear weapons, and reconfigured the global balance of power. The Allies' eventual victory ended the totalitarian regimes of Hitler and Mussolini, while also redefining Japan's future. Yet it simultaneously opened a new chapter in world affairs, dominated by superpower rivalry and the quest to rebuild entire continents. In the context of our survey of the world's most significant conflicts, World War II stands as a grim testament to humanity's capacity for both technological progress and unparalleled destruction.

Final Thoughts

With Chapters Nineteen and Twenty, our book arrives at the mid-20th century, having traversed a vast historical landscape of major wars—from the earliest organized conflicts through the ancient world, medieval struggles, the Napoleonic era, 19th-century upheavals, and finally World War I and World War II. These last two global catastrophes forever altered international relations, warfare technology, and societal norms. While this is the end of our exploration for now, the legacies of these wars continue to shape our world. By studying their causes, courses, and consequences, we gain insights into the forces that drive nations to fight—and the fragile peace that can result when war's lessons go unheeded.

Help Us Share Your Thoughts!

Dear reader,

Thank you for spending your time with this book. We hope it brought you enjoyment and a few new ideas to think about. If there was anything that didn't work for you, or if you have suggestions on how we can improve, please let us know at **kontakt@skriuwer.com**. Your feedback means a lot to us and helps us make our books even better.

If you enjoyed this book, we would be very grateful if you left a review on the site where you purchased it. Your review not only helps other readers find our books, but also encourages us to keep creating more stories and materials that you'll love.

By choosing Skriuwer, you're also supporting **Frisian**—a minority language mainly spoken in the northern Netherlands. Although **Frisian** has a rich history, the number of speakers is shrinking, and it's at risk of dying out. Your purchase helps fund resources to preserve and promote this language, such as educational programs and learning tools. If you'd like to learn more about Frisian or even start learning it yourself, please visit **www.learnfrisian.com**.

Thank you for being part of our community. We look forward to sharing more books with you in the future.

Warm regards,
The Skriuwer Team

www.ingramcontent.com/pod-product-compliance
Lightning Source LLC
LaVergne TN
LVHW012105070526
838202LV00056B/5626